Early in 1929, with the publication of Dashiell Hammett's novel, *Red Harvest*, a new kind of mystery fiction was launched in America: tough, unsentimental, uncompromisingly realistic, reflecting the violence of its time. Four more books—*The Dain Curse*, *The Maltese Falcon*, *The Glass Key* and *The Thin Man*—established Hammett as "a creator of the first rank," a master who shaped and developed the hard-boiled school of crime fiction.

Here is the first full-length study dealing with the dynamic writer whose characters—from the Continental Op, that fat, nameless San Francisco sleuth, through private eye Sam Spade and thin man Nick Charles to comic-strip hero Secret Agent X-9—have become part of our national folklore. In creating what Ellery Queen terms "the first one hundred percent American . . . truly *native* detective story," Hammett brilliantly defined the troubled aspects of his age, a period of open criminal warfare, poverty and festering political corruption.

A critical, moody, stern, complex man whose personal code of ethics was as unyielding as the fictional code his characters lived by, he laid a hard-boiled veneer over the despair of citizens who were disinherited and disenchanted, and forged an objective prose style which revolutionized the genre.

Tracing Dashiell Hammett's violent years as a Pinkerton detective, this book tells how Hammett translated his on-the-job experiences into realistic crime tales for the pages of *Black Mask*, bringing the gritty argot of the streets into print, honestly portraying thugs, con men, stoolies, cops and professional killers.

Fighting lung disease and alcoholism, gambling away his money in Hollywood, surviving the dark months of a federal prison term as a victim of

Angeles Times and published essays and checklists on Ernest Hemingway, Ray Bradbury and other popular literary figures. In 1960 the American Library Association selected one of his books, *Adventure on Wheels*, as outstanding in its genre. Within the mystery field, Mr. Nolan has written articles on Raymond Chandler and Ian Fleming, and his fiction has achieved honor roll standing in *Best Detective Stories of the Year*. Seventeen of his books have been published around the world over the last decade. His latest novel, *Logan's Run*, was recently purchased for the screen by Metro-Goldwyn-Mayer.

DASHIELL HAMMETT
A Casebook

By William F. Nolan

Adventure on Wheels

Barney Oldfield

Phil Hill: Yankee Champion

John Huston: King Rebel

Men of Thunder

Dashiell Hammett: A Casebook

Dashiell Hammett

A CASEBOOK

William F. Nolan

with an introduction
by
PHILIP DURHAM

A LIONSHEAD BOOK

McNALLY & LOFTIN, *Publishers*
Santa Barbara

Library of Congress Catalog Card Number 68–8393

Manufactured in the United States of America by Heritage Printers, Inc., Charlotte, N. C.

First printing

For Clifford McCarty

ACKNOWLEDGMENTS

DURING HIS LIFETIME Hammett consistently avoided personal publicity, sharing Faulkner's affinity for a place outside the limelight. He gave few interviews, refusing, in his final illness, the honor of being profiled as part of the *Paris Review* "Writers at Work" series. *The Cyclopedia of World Authors* reports, under biographical references, "There is no extended biographical study or criticism."

Thus, Dashiell Hammett has long been considered "the mystery man of mystery fiction." This book marks the first full-length attempt to cover his career. It is not, nor does it pretend to be, a definitive treatment. Until Lillian Hellman, who controls his estate, releases the full Hammett Papers, including now-restricted letters, unpublished manuscripts, and various personal documents, no comprehensive study can be successfully undertaken. Yet, for librarians, university students, crime buffs, and readers who seek collected information on Samuel Dashiell Hammett and the school of hard-boiled fiction he established, this book, with its first published listing of work by and about him in all fields, should prove of worth. Hopefully, it will stimulate re-evaluation of a creatively important, critically neglected American writer, a prophet of violence in a faithless age, who transcended the boundaries of his chosen field to win a permanent place in world literature.

I am indebted to a number of generous individuals for special aid in this project: to William Sloane and Helen Stewart, both of Rutgers University Press, for initial encouragement; to Clifford McCarty and Shelly Lowenkopf for numerous personal contributions; to specialist-collector Ned Guymon—and to Tyrus G. Harmsen of Occidental College—for providing me with a copy of the early, unpublished "Thin Man"; to William J. Clark for valuable check-list information; to Philip Durham, Wilbur Smith, and the UCLA staff for help with my *Black Mask* research; to Albert S. Samuels for his early-day anecdotes about Hammett; to John Stanley of San Francisco's *Chronicle* for "morgue" data; to correspondents Ron Goulart, Joseph Blotner, Matthew Bruccoli, W. T. Ballard, Henry Klinger, E. H. Mundell, Jr., Joseph Willicombe (of King Features), Erle Stanley Gardner, Al Hubin (of *The Armchair Detective*), Herbert Ruhm, Charles Burt, and George F. O'Neill (of Pinkerton's, Inc.); and to Jim Harmon for sharing old radio memories; to Allen Rivkin, Sanora Babb, Kam Lytton, Ray Bradbury, and Frank Gruber for local support; to David Madden for allowing me advance access to material from his edited collection *Tough Guy Writers of the Thirties*; to all those I have quoted in my text, particularly Frederic Dannay and Lillian Hellman; and to the hard-working staff members of the Library of Congress, the New York Public Library, the Academy of Motion Picture Arts and Sciences Library of Hollywood—and with special thanks to William J. McNally and Kenneth Millar.

WILLIAM F. NOLAN

Los Angeles, California

"By heaven, man, we are turned round and round in this world, like yonder windlass, and Fate is the handspike."

——Herman Melville,
Moby Dick.

"I see him . . . a little man going forward day after day through mud and blood and death and deceit—as callous and brutal and cynical as necessary—toward a dim goal, with nothing to push or pull him to it except he's been hired to reach it."

——Dashiell Hammett,
on the Continental Op.

CONTENTS

INTRODUCTION

DASHIELL HAMMETT was a popular writer; two of his novels—*The Maltese Falcon* and *The Thin Man*—sold more than two and one half million copies. But these sales did not compare with the multi-million sales of Mickey Spillane and Erle Stanley Gardner. Because Hammett was more than a popular writer. Hammett would have written of society and of the men in it and of its values whether or not his stories proved to be popular.

The chief characteristic of Hammett's stories was the hero, the hard-boiled private eye. The kind of hero who, almost a commonplace until the 1930s, is almost an anachronism in the 1960s. He was not an existentialist, for he made choices and felt responsible for individuals. He was not a nihilist, for although he saw the bottom of life, he did not believe that life was entirely empty, that all men were absurd, that the universe was necessarily indifferent, that death had to be meaningless. He fought to live, and he challenged death to keep others alive. John Paterson once wrote of Hammett's hard-boiled hero that he "is, in the final analysis, the apotheosis of every-man of good will who, alienated by the values of his time, seeks desperately and mournfully to live without shame, to live without compromise to his integrity."

The hero about whom Hammett wrote was a part of a

continuous tradition that began on the frontier in the early part of the nineteenth century. This American literary hero started with Brom Bones in the pages of Washington Irving, continued in the tales of Augustus Longstreet, Charles Webber, Joseph Baldwin, and Alfred Arrington, appeared constantly in the dime novels of the House of Beadle and Adams, and was ready-made for such "Western" writers of the twentieth century as Owen Wister and Zane Grey. By the time Hammett picked him up in the pages of *Black Mask,* in the early 1920s, his heroic characteristics were clearly established: courage, physical strength, indestructibility, indifference to danger and death, a knightly attitude, celibacy, a measure of violence, and a sense of justice.

Black Mask, for which Dashiell Hammett began his writing career in 1922, was the famous pulp magazine that writers of private-eye stories hoped to make. According to Lester Dent, one of Hammett's contemporaries, *Black Mask* came into being during that "brief wonderful time when American literature was endowed with the most effective training ground in all history—the pulp magazine." The name "Hammett" has become synonymous with *Black Mask,* and surely Hammett was the leader of the *Black Mask* School—a school that in recent years has been more and more recognized (both in America and abroad) as having influenced American literature. Dozens of Hammett's stories and all of his novels except *The Thin Man* originally appeared in *Black Mask.*

Dashiell Hammett's heroes—the Continental Op, Sam Spade, Ned Beaumont—were violent, but their violence was not merely that of sensationalism. It was rather a kind of meaningful violence, sometimes an explicit description and implicit criticism of a corrupt society. Many Americans lost faith in the society of the 1920s, and Hammett's heroes tried both to expose the corruptness and to speak for men who, questioning the values of society, needed to be assured

that somewhere—if only on the pages of a pulp magazine—there were heroes who cared.

William Nolan points out that like Ernest Hemingway—who was experimenting with writing techniques at the same time—Hammett was trying to make events truer than life. What is truth and what is real become so only when it is creatively imagined. Beginning with his earliest stories Hammett worked with plot, trying to keep it from becoming too obviously stereotyped. He created a protagonist, a common man who could be believed in. He used the theme of the rugged individualist righting social wrongs. And he concentrated on the objective, hard-boiled style, attempting to make it as action-packed as possible.

Although Hammett's heroes could see through falsehoods, they could understand human frailty, and they responded to pleas such as those made by Brigid O'Shaughnessy in *The Maltese Falcon*:

> I know this isn't fair of me. But be generous, Mr. Spade, don't ask me to be fair. You're strong, you're resourceful, you're brave. You can spare me some of that strength and resourcefulness and courage, surely. Help me because I need help so badly, and because if you don't where will I find anyone who can, no matter how willing? Help me. I've no right to ask you to help me blindly, but I do ask you. Be generous, Mr. Spade. You can help me. Help me.

And Spade did help, but he also had to be fair. When he found out that Brigid had killed his partner—although he loved Brigid and hated his partner—fairness took over. He gave her seven reasons, all code rules, why he had to turn her in. Then he added, "Well, if I send you over I'll be sorry as hell—I'll have some rotten nights—but that'll pass." So justice was done, and the hero went on to the next case.

This book is the first attempt to do a full-length treat-

ment of Dashiell Hammett. I am sure that it will lead the way to many more, for Hammett is worth it. And when his estate releases the Hammett material, those writers who take up the fascinating life and letters of Dashiell Hammett will have to begin with this book by William Nolan. I gladly go with the author of this study when he writes: "Hopefully, it will stimulate re-evaluation of a creatively important, critically neglected American writer, a prophet of violence in a faithless age, who transcended the boundaries of his chosen field to win a permanent place in world literature."

PHILIP DURHAM

Los Angeles, California

DASHIELL HAMMETT
A Casebook

1

THE MURDEROUS LANDSCAPE

THE DETECTIVE STORY WAS BORN in April of 1841, with the publication of "The Murders in the Rue Morgue" in the pages of *Graham's Magazine*. Inspired by *Memoires*, the popular autobiography of detective Francois Vidocq published twelve years earlier, Edgar Allan Poe created his classic fictional sleuth, C. Auguste Dupin, forming the first link in a chain which continues to lengthen today, more than a century and a quarter later.

Charles Dickens, with *Bleak House* in 1853, brought detection to England, while Wilkie Collins carried forward the Poe ingredients. The next stage was French, with Emile Gaboriau's first detective novel, *L'Affaire Lerouge*, appearing in 1866. In 1878 Anna Katharine Green published *The Leavenworth Case*, which brought detective fiction back to America. Poe's influence was brilliantly extended by Arthur Conan Doyle, whose classic Sherlock Holmes adventure, *A Study in Scarlet*, in 1887, solidified the form at the level of the deductive puzzle. A host of other writers developed the mystery story, including Mary Roberts Rinehart, Melville Davisson Post, Arthur B. Reeve, G.K. Chesterton, E. C. Bentley, A.E.W. Mason, H.C. Bailey, Freeman Wills Crofts, Agatha Christie and (beginning in 1926) the enormously popular Willard Huntington Wright, writing the Philo Vance novels as S.S. Van Dine.

With the publication of Dashiell Hammett's novel, *Red Harvest*, early in 1929, a new style of detective fiction was launched in America: bitter, tough, unsentimental, uncompromisingly realistic, reflecting the violence of its time. Hammett's savagely dialogued, bare-knuckle approach established a school which quickly abandoned staid English tradition. Murder bounced from the tea garden to the back alley, and the polite gentleman sleuth gave way to the hard-boiled private eye, a man of action who fought crime by his own rules, yet who followed a rigid personal code: a knight in a trenchcoat, who carried a .38 and knew how to use it, who punished hoods as much as they punished him, who worked outside society for the overall good of society.

Hammett brought him to raw life, blazing a fictional path which other highly talented suspense novelists such as Raymond Chandler, Ian Fleming, and Ross Macdonald would follow and extend. Fleming, author of the James Bond books, who openly credited Hammett's influence on his own work, wrote of Chandler: "Dashiell Hammett was Chandler's first love among thriller writers and [he said] he'd learned most from Hammett and Hemingway."

Chandler himself cited Hammett as the "ace performer," who "gave murder back to the kind of people that commit it. . . . He put these people down on paper as they are, and he made them talk and think in the language they customarily used for these purposes. Hammett's style, at its best . . . could say almost anything."

This style was actually a seed-down from Twain, who within the character of Huck Finn employed "living speech," writing in the language of the people for maximum clarity and deep-root communication.

Dashiell Hammett has been called "the Hemingway of detective fiction," but the term has not always been employed in a complimentary sense. Several critics have dismissed Hammett as simply an extension of Hemingway,

declaring that he openly imitated that author's terse, understated style and dialogue.

This charge merits examination.

Ernest Hemingway did not publish a book in the United States until late 1925, when *In Our Time,* his first collection of stories, was published by Scribners. By then Hammett had been writing professionally for three years. Only one Hemingway story had been published in this country prior to 1925, "My Old Man" (included in *The Best Short Stories of 1923*). This tale was heavily influenced by Sherwood Anderson, reflecting little of the controlled, lean Hemingway of later years, and thus could not possibly have been a factor in Hammett's development.

It is fascinating to consider that as a near-starving Hemingway labored in a Paris loft during 1922–1923, carving out a muscular, objective prose style which was to become the major influence on mainstream writing, so labored a near-starving Hammett in a San Francisco hotel room, carving out precisely the same prose style, which was to alter completely the fabric of America's popular crime fiction.

Both men, working independently, became masters of objective realism. In linking these two writers, essayist Walter Blair finds a common emotional background. "Wounded by the war and unhappy in the postwar world . . . contemptuous of many pre-World War I standards . . . both were battered by disillusionment and cynicism, and both created worlds and characters justifying their attitude." Later, as each read the other's work, a cross-influence may have developed, creating mutual benefit. (André Gide was to say of Hammett: "[His] dialogues . . . can be compared only with the best in Hemingway.") Widespread circulation of "The Killers," printed in 1927, may have influenced Hammett's fiction of that period. Yet it is equally reasonable to conjecture that 1929's *Red Harvest* might

well have had a hand in shaping *To Have and Have Not,* published in 1937 (the same year Hammett appeared at a pro-Loyalist gathering organized by Hemingway in Hollywood).

Despite Philip Young's assertion that, of the tough detective school, Raymond Chandler was "the only member of it Hemingway . . . could read," we know (from *Death in the Afternoon*) that Hammett's *The Dain Curse* was a Hemingway favorite. Thus, cross-influence was certainly possible.

Hammett's prose-fiction career was of brief duration, extending from 1922 into early 1934, but during these twelve years he produced some seventy-five stories and novels, including such best-selling books as *The Maltese Falcon, The Glass Key* and *The Thin Man.* The bulk of his fiction was written for *Black Mask,* but Hammett also contributed original stories to more than fifteen other publications. His post-1934 low-level production added nothing to his critical reputation, yet he remained one of the most famous and well-paid writers of his generation. Few artists have ever reached a wider mass audience with work for films, comic strips, radio, and television. Reprints and overseas distribution added to his popularity, and between 1934 and 1961 his work sold over four million copies in paperback editions. Two of his novels have achieved all-time best seller status (among the 600-plus books published since 1895 which have surpassed the million-copy mark). *The Thin Man* sold 1,400,000 copies through 1965, and *The Maltese Falcon* reached a total, in the same period, of 1,100,000 copies. In overall sales, Hammett follows crimedom's "big three": Spillane, Fleming, and Gardner.

Although he lived to the age of sixty-six, all of Hammett's important, tradition-breaking work was behind him by his fortieth birthday. (In marked contrast, Chandler was fifty when his first novel was released, and he published his

most mature effort, *The Long Goodbye,* at the age of sixty-five.)

Hammett's overall achievement, however, cannot be disputed.

As Anthony Boucher pointed out, "In only a decade of creative activity Hammett exerted an influence on the American detective story greater than that of any author since Poe."

Dashiell Hammett was a critical, moody, stern, complex man whose personal code was as unyielding as the fictional code his characters lived by. That he created almost strictly within the crime genre is no accident; he was a realist, and his rough-and-tumble life as a detective provided the background out of which he drew his characters and stories. It is fortunate for literature that he chose to become a Pinkerton man. Unlike many of his contemporaries who used the field without a working knowledge of it, plotting their fanciful crimes between tea sessions in the parlor, Hammett, in creating what Ellery Queen called "the first 100 percent American . . . truly native detective story," was able to bring the gritty argot of the streets into print, to portray authentically the thugs, hobos, molls, stoolies, gunmen, and cops, political bosses and crooked clients, allowing them to talk and behave on paper as they had talked and behaved in Hammett's manhunting years.

"The contemporary novelist's job is to take pieces of life and arrange them on paper," Hammett once declared. "And the more direct their passage from street to paper the more lifelike they should turn out . . . [he] needs to make what is set down seem truly contemporary, to give the impression of things happening here and now, to force upon the reader a feeling of immediacy. . . . The novelist must know how things happen—not how they are remembered in later years—and he must write them down that way."

Critic Graham McInnes found that "Hammett's prose represents the irreducible essence of action and emotion. It has, in its own sphere, the polish and meat of an essay by Bacon or a poem by Donne, both of whom also lived in an age of violence and transition."

America, in the Twenties and Thirties, was receptive to the detective as a modern frontiersman, battling social and economic evils, trusting no one but himself (and Hammett's detective doubted even himself in *Red Harvest*), seeing corruption on a daily level with an unflinching eye. Critic Leslie Fiedler, who did not rank Hammett as a major artist, nonetheless recognized his place in crime literature: "As created by Hammett, the blameless [detective] is also the honest proletarian, illuminating by contrast the decadent society of the rich."

Hammett projected his dark visions with a fidelity and style deeply rooted in the era. As Philip Durham says, "Hammett's private eye speaks for men who had lost faith in the values of their society during war, gangsterism and depression."

Herbert Ruhm finds "the Hammett hero has no future and what little past he has is not personal but experimental: he has run into a man, been in a city, and what the city looks like is unimportant . . . he has no ambition . . . no home, no wife, no children. . . . He has no roots . . . [and lives] a bleak existence in a cold world . . . a world of chance . . . a blind universe . . . with all values but competence and loyalty gone. . . . The left-wing periodicals of the Thirties had given Hammett no play . . . perhaps because his work suggests no solution: no mass-action . . . no individual salvation . . . no Emersonian reconciliation and transcendence."

Edmund Wilson, in recalling the two decades between the major wars, found society "ridden by an all-pervasive feeling of guilt and by a feel of impending disaster which

it seemed hopeless to try to avert." In Wilson's view, nobody was guiltless, nobody safe.

Hammett brilliantly defined the troubled aspects of this period of open criminal warfare, poverty, and festering political corruption. He laid a hard-boiled veneer over the despair and anguish of citizens who were disinherited and disenchanted. Clam up, he told them. Stay tough. Never show your tears. Don't back down to anybody. Learn to take it. Then maybe, just *maybe*, you can survive. Go soft and you're finished. Stay cold, detached, hard, outwardly emotionless—and you've got a chance. Hammett believed in this philosophy, practiced it all his life. In his last days, critically ill and often in pain, he was asked by the woman who loved him if he wanted to talk about it. "No," he told her. "My only chance is not to talk about it."

In 1923, for *Black Mask*, Hammett created his Continental Op in this hard, unsentimental mold. And six years later, Sam Spade became the Op's natural successor, both of them men who could be hurt but wouldn't show it, wouldn't talk about it. Hammett did not glorify toughness; he honestly portrayed it—firmly separating his work from the bizarre Spillane school of rampant sex and sadism which followed.

Crime, from theft to murder, in a Hammett story, never mattered as much as the characters who committed it; lawbreaking and violence were the natural byproducts of their environment. The clipped, rapid-fire dialogue formed the author's "style"—yet Hammett was simply attempting to reproduce, in dramatic terms, the lean speech of the man who says nothing more than he has to.

The hard-boiled novel may be traced through the naturalistic prose of Zola into the hard realism of Norris, Dreiser, London, and Crane. Many writers of the Thirties mined this vein: O'Hara, Cain, Steinbeck, Dos Passos, Caldwell, Faulkner, Lardner, Farrell, Algren, and West—

but no other writer within the field treated the crime genre with the lean, tough, natural authority of Dashiell Hammett. The hard-boiled detective novel was his special domain, and his contribution to it remains unsurpassed.

Hammett's protagonists usually combined the cynic and the idealist. They existed in a Darwinian-Nietzschean sense, their carefully-preserved hardness allowing them to survive. It formed their shield against a threatening world (Melville's "appalling ocean"). No one could buy them off or bluff them; they were capable of killing, but as the frontier sheriff kills, in line of duty against a larger evil. Bitterness and cynicism came with the territory. They moved warily through a fragmented landscape in which sudden death existed as part of the scenery, adjusting their morals to fit the dangers and corruption encountered enroute. They learned to keep themselves under tight control; rigid self-discipline was a necessary art. Yet, idealistically, they hoped for a better world, worked doggedly toward it. Hammett gave such characters organic form; he made them coldly, logically alive to the reader. We believe what the Op tells us because his behavior and attitudes are inevitable within his environment. He is, as John Paterson calls him, "the denizen of the dark borderland between good and evil." Another critic compares him to Jake Barnes and Dick Diver: "Hemingway had his stoic hero [Barnes], Fitzgerald his ravaged idealist [Diver] and Hammett had his detective . . . a hard-headed realist . . . who turned the human quest into a manhunt and bulldozed his way through desperation with a gun in one fist and a blackjack in the other."

The Op, of course, projected much more than violence; Hammett was zealous in utilizing full agency procedure: the Op questioned anyone and everyone connected with the crime at hand, slowly collected bits of verbal and physical evidence (from the shape of a man's ear, through a woman's tone of voice, to a careful study of several inter-

secting avenues); he patiently shadowed suspects, examined police lab reports, requested extra help from his agency whenever he thought the case merited it. He did not panic or bow to pressure or persuasion; he was never in a hurry. With Sisyphus, he knew his task would never really be done, the mountain of evil was too high. He must go on, from case to case, endlessly treading his hellish landscape.

According to Donald Phelps, the Op's "pragmatic calm, shrewdness, and monolithic fortitude enable us to see, in relief, the crass, murderous, tumbled universe which Hammett has rendered."

2

A YOUNG PINKERTON

DASHIELL HAMMETT'S FICTION WAS CREATED from the reality of his past—and the scars he carried on his body were earned on the job during his violent years as a Pinkerton agent.

In 1850, Allan Pinkerton, a big-nosed, hard-muscled immigrant from Scotland, gave up his position as a detective with the Chicago police to launch Pinkerton's National Detective Agency. He often rode shotgun on stages, and became famous for capturing Frank Reno, the elusive train robber. It was Allan Pinkerton who originated the term "private eye." For his trademark, he used a drawing of a wide-open human eye, combined with the words, "We Never Sleep." Pinkerton operatives shot it out with drunken badmen, infiltrated Confederate lines in the service of Lincoln, pursued lawbreakers into the jungles of Central America (a fact which doubtless inspired Hammett's first *Black Mask* crime tale in 1922), policed boxing matches, traced stolen gold, and assisted law enforcement officers across the nation.

Along with the population and the crime rate, the agency kept expanding and, in the larger cities, a common method of recruitment included the placement of subtly worded advertisements.

"An enigmatic want ad in a Baltimore paper took me

into the employ of Pinkerton's," Hammett stated. "Prior to this I was the unsatisfactory and unsatisfied employee of various railroads, stock brokers, machine manufacturers, canners. . . . Usually I was fired."

Hammett's early years were chaotic—and toughening. At fourteen he had left the Baltimore Polytechnic Institute "after a fraction of a year of high school" to take a job as messenger boy for the Baltimore and Ohio Railroad, never returning to formal studies. His knock-about education was obtained as freight clerk, stevedore, timekeeper, yard-man, laborer, and as a nail-machine operator in a box factory. He kept on the move, was easily bored by routine, refused to conform. Working for the railroad, he arrived late each day for a week. Finally, his angry employer fired him. Hammett didn't object. Walking out, he was stopped. "Give me your word it won't happen again, and I'll let you stay on," the man told him. Hammett hesitated, shook his head. No, he could not give his word. He would not lie to keep a job. The non-conformist pattern was already established; from the outset, Samuel Dashiell Hammett was his own man, following a private vision.

"I was born in St. Mary's County, Maryland, between the Potomac and Patuxent rivers on May 27, 1894," he related. "I was a very fat baby, but grew up tall and thin. The only remarkable thing about my family was that there were, on my mother's side, sixteen army men of France who never saw a battle. That, and the fact that my grandmother went to the movies every afternoon: she loved Wallace Reid."

A Southern Catholic, raised in Baltimore and Philadelphia, the son of Richard Thomas Hammett and Annie Bond Hammett, he was Scottish and French. The family name was De Chiel, with "Dashiell" an Americanized version, the accent falling on the second syllable.

Hammett once recalled that his mother had given him two memorable pieces of advice: "Never go out in a boat

without oars—and don't waste your time on a woman who can't cook."

Just out of his teens, having answered the Pinkerton want ad, he was hired as an agent in Baltimore, and subsequently worked in many other cities. The new job was exciting, stimulating, a challenge to young Hammett, and his boredom vanished. This profession demanded wit, patience, adaptability and nerve; each case was different, each day offered fresh adventure. He won his first promotion by capturing a man who had stolen a Ferris wheel.

"Detective work is often ridiculous," Hammett declared. "There's great humor in it. I was shadowing a man who finally got lost in the country—and I ended up stepping forward to direct him back to the city. On another occasion, the situation was reversed: I was trying to peer into the upper story of a roadhouse when part of the porch crumbled under me and I fell, spraining an ankle. The proprietor of the roadhouse gave me water to bathe it in. . . . Then there was the operative I knew who was looking for pickpockets at the Havre de Grace race track—and had his wallet lifted."

Hammett also remembered that foul weather had once won him a conviction. He was transporting a prisoner from a ranch in Gilt Edge, Montana, to Lewistown, Idaho, in winter, when their car broke down. The prisoner, who had stubbornly declared his innocence, wore only thin coveralls. He'd been captured without a coat. Hammett was warmly attired. As they sat through the long, frosted night awaiting help, the man got colder and more miserable by the hour. "At dawn," says Hammett, "his morale was so low he made a full confession."

False identity was often required of a Pinkerton agent. In Oregon, Hammett introduced himself as the secretary of the Civic Purity League, hoping to obtain information on a suspect. The information wasn't there, but before he could make his exit he was cornered by a dedicated woman

purist and subjected to a long discourse on the erotic effects of cigarettes upon young ladies. Another case required Hammett to spend three months in a hospital in conversational pursuit of a suspect in the adjoining bed.

But the dangers were real. Hammett carried a gun and used it. Lillian Hellman recalls "the bad cuts on his legs and the indentation in his head from being scrappy with criminals."

The Pinkerton years were interrupted by an enlistment in the Motor Ambulance Corps in June of 1918. Hammett became a sergeant, but was frustrated at being assigned to a post just twenty miles from his home in Baltimore. In camp, an attack of influenza led to tuberculosis, and he began a long battle with the lung disease.

Out of the service, in July of 1919, he felt strong enough to resume detective work. His biggest assignment during this period involved the Nicky Arnstein bond-theft case.

Nick was an ambitious gambler, a dapper, elegant man who wore monogrammed twill-silk pajamas, kept seven toothbrushes in his bathroom and owned a stable of racing thoroughbreds. In 1915 he was convicted on a swindling charge and sentenced to Sing Sing for two years. Out of prison, he became the second husband of comedienne Fanny Brice in New York.

By February of 1920 Nick was again in trouble with the law. He was called the mastermind of a plot to steal $5,000,000 in securities from Wall Street brokers. A newspaper account stated: "Detectives seek Arnstein, known to police as a member of the notorious Gondorf band . . . who fleeced scores of men in this city for sums aggregating upward of $1,000,000."

Dashiell Hammett was among the detectives seeking Arnstein. Nick had shaved his mustache and disappeared. The Pinkerton office told Hammett he was to shadow Fanny Brice, in the hope she would contact her missing husband.

"For weeks I tailed her, with no luck," stated Hammett. "Then suddenly Nick turned himself in, and was convicted. In later years Fanny and I became great friends, but I never told her I was one of the gumshoes involved in that case."

Shadowing a suspect, Hammett claimed, was relatively simple. There are four rules: keep behind the subject; never attempt to hide from him; act naturally, no matter the situation; never meet his eye. "You simply saunter along somewhere within sight of your subject and, barring bad breaks, the only thing that can make you lose him is over-anxiety on your part. Even a clever criminal may be shadowed for weeks without suspecting it. I knew one operative who shadowed a wily old forger for more than three months without arousing his suspicion. I myself trailed one for six weeks, riding trains and making half a dozen small towns with him; and I wasn't exactly inconspicuous, standing an inch or so over six feet. You don't worry about a suspect's face. Tricks of carriage, ways of wearing clothes, general outline, individual mannerisms—all as seen from the rear—are much more important to the shadow than faces."

Hammett ranged the states for Pinkerton: he arrested a smooth talking forger in Pasco, Washington; he rejected an offer to enter the narcotics trade with a pusher in San Diego; he shadowed a man suspected of being an enemy agent in Washington, D.C.; he ran down a window-smasher in Stockton, California; he studied the art of faked prints with Wesley Turner, of the Spokane police identification bureau; he worked with a stool pigeon to obtain criminal data in Butte, Montana; he tracked down a fugitive swindler in Seattle.

"Going from the larger cities out into the remote rural communities," he reported, "one finds a steadily decreasing percentage of crimes that have to do with money and a

proportionate increase in the frequency of sex as a criminal motive."

Hammett became quite knowledgeable in matters of criminal lore: "The pick-pocket has no status in the world of crime. Pocket-picking is the easiest to master of all the criminal trades. Anyone who is not crippled can become adept in a day."

Or: "The value of fingerprints is over-rated. Even where the criminal makes no attempt to efface the prints of his fingers, but leaves them all over the scene of the crime, the chances are about one in ten of finding a print that is sufficiently clear to be of any value."

Or: "Of all the men embezzling from their employers with whom I have had contact, I can't remember a dozen who drank or had any of the vices in which bonding companies are so interested."

Or: "House burglary is probably the poorest paid trade in the world. I have never known anyone to make a living at it. But for that matter few criminals of any class are self-supporting unless they toil at something legit between times. Most of them live on their women."

Or: "Of all the nationalities, the Greek is the most difficult to convict. He simply denies everything, no matter how conclusive the proof may be; and nothing so impresses a jury as a bare statement of fact, regardless of the fact's inherent improbability or obvious absurdity in the face of overwhelming contrary evidence."

Manhunting eventually took its toll on Hammett's health, and by mid-1920 he was again bedded down with lung trouble, his tuberculosis re-activated. An Indian school on Puyallup Road on the fringes of Tacoma, Washington, had been converted into a lung hospital—and Hammett entered as a disabled veteran of World War I.

He shared a room with a "kid from Snohomish," who liked cards. They would drape the window with a blanket

and play poker into the dawn, sipping bootleg whiskey. This improved their spirits if not their health—and overnight passes to Seattle were also obtainable from the corruptible head nurse. The ex-detective had brought along a Pinkerton blackjack, and this intrigued another patient, Whitey Kaiser, a muscleman from Alaska.

"Whitey borrowed the blackjack one night and returned it the next morning with ten bucks. Then I read about a man being slugged and robbed of a hundred and eighty dollars on the Puyallup Road the night before. I showed the clip to Whitey, who said people who were robbed always exaggerated the amounts."

Boredom set in, and Hammett devised a plan to "liven up the place." He enlisted the aid of a huge ex-Marine named Bizzarri. They began openly insulting each other, growing more surly with each passing day. Hammett called Bizzarri strong names—and the names were returned, with elaborations. The nurses became alarmed, begging them to shake hands, to forget their bitterness. No, said Hammett, the only way to end it was man-to-man, fist-to-fist. A slugout.

"We went into the yard one afternoon for our final violent showdown, with the whole staff trailing nervously behind us," recalled Hammett. "After a couple of wild swings we couldn't control ourselves. We broke down and began to laugh. The gag was shot."

The staff had endured enough of Hammett's pranks—and he was sent south, to an Army hospital near San Diego built on the site of old Camp Kearney. On the train to California, in order to raise smoking money, Hammett and Whitey Kaiser sold a packet of harmless white powders (prescribed to Kaiser for a kidney infection) as "real stuff" to a pair of self-declared hopheads. ("And they got—or *thought* they got—a good bang out of those pills all the way to San Diego!")

The routine at the new hospital was more rigidly enforced, and when Whitey put away several bottles of high-

alcohol-content patent medicines and slugged his doctor he was promptly shipped out. But Hammett did not mourn him; he was busy with an attractive nurse named Josie, among other interests.

Located on the edge of the desert, the hospital offered varied delights. Hammett recalled that he made pets of horned toads and staged Gila monster battles in an abandoned boxcar, pitting the ugly-tempered lizards against rattlesnakes. ("The Gila monsters always won, but most of the sucker money backed the rattlers.") And, as his health improved, he was able to take off for Tijuana for an occasional border weekend.

But Josie came first, and on December 27, 1920 they were married: Josephine A. Dolan, of Anaconda, Montana, became Mrs. Samuel D. Hammett.

At twenty-six, the detective had a wife.

By May of 1921 Hammett had obtained his release from the hospital, his file marked "maximum improvement reached." Actually, his disease had not run its course, but he was well enough to resume his career.

The Hammetts visited Spokane, then headed for northern California for an interim stop.

"That stop lasted eight years," Hammett declared. "We didn't intend to stay more than two months before returning to my home in Baltimore, but Baltimore was a pretty dull town, and San Francisco looked like fun."

Hammett joined the local branch of the Pinkerton Agency, and by September was involved in the notorious Arbuckle rape case in San Francisco.

The basic facts are well known. Roscoe "Fatty" Arbuckle, famed silent screen comic, arranged a party at the St. Francis Hotel replete with two cases of bootleg gin, a department store model, several other guests from Los Angeles and a young actress, Virginia Rappe. The party was loud and rough, with Arbuckle clowning broadly for the amused Miss Rappe. But a passing maid heard screams

from the suite, and the manager was called. The Rappe girl was hurriedly taken to another room for medical examination. Her trouble was diagnosed as a ruptured bladder. Four days later she died of peritonitis resulting from the rupture.

Arbuckle was blamed in the girl's death. It was said he attempted to rape her on the bed, pressing his 300-pound body upon her in brutal fashion. The actor denied this charge, but was brought to trial. Hammett was one of several detectives assigned to the case.

"The whole thing was a frame-up, arranged by some of the corrupt local newspaper boys," he declared. "Arbuckle was good copy, so they set him up for a fall. It took three trials to clear him. In the second one there was an interesting sidelight having to do with forged fingerprints. The defense introduced an expert from Los Angeles who testified that any print could be faked, and that he had deceived an assembly of his official colleagues with a set of forged prints. I later used this as the basis for a short story."

Writing was beginning to infiltrate Hammett's life; between cases he was turning out bits of verse, true-crime "fillers," jotting down notations from his experiences as a manhunter.

"I was beginning to sour on being a detective," declared Hammett. "The excitement was no longer there, and losing a trip to Australia put the cap on it for me."

A boat out of Australia, on a round trip to California, had reported a theft at sea. More than $200,000 in gold was missing, and the ship's captain wanted the vessel searched when it docked in San Francisco. The insurance company was a client of the Pinkerton Agency, who sent Hammett out with another operative to meet the boat and search it. They found nothing. The Pinkerton office decided to send Hammett back to Australia on board in the hope that he could turn up the missing treasure.

"I was delighted. I'd dreamed of a trip to Australia. It sounded great."

Hammett packed, got ready to embark—then made one final round of the boat. On impulse, he climbed to the top of a smoke stack, peered over the edge. And there it was. Gold. The search was over.

"I was furious with myself," admitted Hammett. "Why couldn't I have discovered the gold one day out to sea? I'd lost my trip. I'd also lost my desire to remain with Pinkerton."

He collected the gold, had it transported back to the agency, and turned in his resignation.

But he had nothing saved, and needed another job.

Hammett placed an ad in the San Francisco *Chronicle*, asking for "any kind of honest work." In it, he enumerated his former occupations, from warehouseman to detective, ending with the words "and I can write."

Albert S. Samuels, who owned a small jewelry store on Market Street, needed a man to turn out newspaper ad copy, and recalls that a friend from the *Chronicle* brought Hammett into the store and introduced him as "your new advertising manager." Samuels read Hammett's ad and hired him immediately.

"He'd write copy for me all day, then go home to his apartment and drink during most of the night, sobering up enough to report in the next morning," recalls Samuels. "Yet he was a man of honor, and he always did fine work. I remember particularly his 'romantic' approach, which was ideal for us."

One such ad depicted two young lovers standing, hand in hand, atop the globe. The girl wore a new diamond ring. Hammett's catch-line read, "A Samuels diamond puts you on top of the world!"

The jaded ex-detective knew that writing ad copy could never satisfy the creative urge for prose which gnawed

at him; Hammett wanted to record his unique experiences on paper, but fiction was a trade he knew nothing about. So he drank, trying to "figure things."

Alcohol and lack of sleep undermined his health, and Hammett's lungs gave way again.

"He had two hemorrhages right in the store," states Samuels. "Once we found him lying unconscious on the floor in a pool of blood. But he couldn't seem to stop the drinking."

Ignoring his wife's pleas, Hammett refused hospitalization. They argued. He left his family (by now they had a two-year-old daughter*) and rented a cheap hotel room in downtown San Francisco.

By God, he would write!

But fiction did not come easy. Despite the fact that he had led an adventurous life Hammett discovered that getting bits and pieces of that life on paper did not automatically guarantee a salable story. Sales were made by professionals who knew their craft; he settled in for his apprenticeship. He would master the art of fiction as he had mastered the art of crime detecting.

* Hammett used her name, Mary Jane Hammett, as a byline for a *Smart Set* story in 1923.

3

BLACK MASK AND THE BIRTH OF AN OP

TWO SEEMINGLY UNRELATED EVENTS in 1920 were to affect profoundly the life of Dashiell Hammett: the publication of the first issue of a new pulp-fiction magazine, in March, and the beginning of Prohibition on the morning of July 16.

Early that year, H. L. Mencken made a decision: he would publish a magazine with fellow luminary George Jean Nathan in the hope of earning a few fast dollars from the burgeoning popular fiction market. For a total investment of five hundred dollars, they launched *The Black Mask* in New York, hiring F. M. Osborne as its editor. Unwilling to associate themselves officially with "a sensational pulp," Mencken and Nathan kept their names off the masthead, yet they were obliged to read incoming manuscripts, as well as edit sections of the magazine.

In April, Mencken wrote a terse note to Ernest Boyd: "*Black Mask* seems to be a success, but the thing has burdened both Nathan and me with disagreeable work."

By 1921 they had sold their brainchild for a profit, much to Mencken's relief. (It continued, under a number of editors, into 1953, when it was absorbed by *Ellery Queen's Mystery Magazine*.)

Pulp fiction was enormously popular in the Twenties. Street & Smith, the leading chain publisher, had brought out *Detective Story Magazine* in 1915 (replacing *Nick Car-*

ter Weekly) and the venture proved very successful. Edgar Wallace began to appear regularly in *Detective Story Magazine*, and by 1920 the pulp-crime genre was firmly established.

Yet the type of detective fiction Hammett would so brilliantly develop had not yet appeared. This was still the Victorian era of cloaked figures, terrified maidens and slow deduction; murder usually took place in musty castles or flowering gardens, in paneled libraries or on fog-shrouded moors. Detectives were tweedy, mustachioed, pompous gentlemen, prone to declarations of Shakespearian intensity, which they zestfully hurled at the guilty. When arresting a murderer, they always wore the proper frock coat and striped trousers, "detectives of exquisite and impossible gentility," as Chandler described them. Even the villains wore top hats.

An excerpt from a 1920 *Black Mask* tale, "The Silvered Sentinel," reflects the ornate, overwritten style of the period: "With a windy shriek De Collyer fell backward upon the bed, the mounting tide of his alcoholic frenzy culminating in an overwhelming wave of insane and blasphemous mouthing, the grim justice of a retributive madness."

Titles were in keeping with this baroque approach: "The Mysterious Shot," "The Uncanny Voice," "The Jest Ironic."

The publication's trademark was a thin black pirate's eyemask with a gun and dirk crossed behind it. And although crime was the main attraction for readers, the magazine did not limit its contents. In addition to "the best Mystery and Detective stories" the editor also promised "the best Romances, the best Love stories, and the best stories of the Occult." (Western tales would soon be added, a feature which would remain part of *Black Mask* for many years.)

By October of 1922 the magazine had a new editor,

George W. Sutton, Jr., who was capably assisted by Harry North. It was Sutton (and North) who first purchased the work of Hammett and Carroll John Daly, the two writers who would shape the hard-boiled hero into what eventually became "the *Black Mask* tradition."

In December of that year, a short 1500-word story was printed under Sutton's editorship, dealing with the adventures of a manhunter who tracked criminals around the world. It was called "The Road Home," and carried the byline of Peter Collinson. The name was false. Collinson was twenty-eight-year-old Samuel Dashiell Hammett, who at that time hoped to retain his real name for poetry.

Hammett once explained how he had come to choose this pseudonym. Criminal slang at the turn of the century included the phrase, "He's a Peter Collins," meaning "He's a nobody." Hammett added "on" to the name, making it, literally, "nobody's son." (In *Red Harvest,* written many years later, Hammett had a dying hood complain, "I got no no more belly left than Peter Collins.")

Told in the third person, "The Road Home" is minor Hammett, but of interest due to its thematic structure. The protagonist is a detective named Hagedorn, hired to bring back a criminal who has led him halfway around the globe. Barnes, the fugitive, captured on a teak boat in the depths of the jungle, offers the detective a share of "one of the richest gem beds in Asia" if he'll throw in with him. Hagedorn refuses the bribe. ("Maybe manhunting isn't the nicest trade in the world, but it's all the trade I've got.") Hagedorn speaks of the wife and family who wait for him in the States. "I'm taking you back to New York," he tells Barnes.

The fugitive leaps into the river, reaches shore and escapes into the jungle, headed for his jewels. The story ends as Hagedorn plunges into the brush after him, thinking about the treasure as he does so. The reader is left with the hint that perhaps the detective *will* be corrupted upon

sighting the jewels. Thus, Hammett's career-long theme of man's basic corruptibility is reflected here, in his *Black Mask* debut.

The style is inconsistent; although Hammett begins his narrative directly with dialogue (a method he often employed to good effect in subsequent work) his description is heavy and derivative: "The dark man in the garb of a native smiled an oily, ingratiating smile and brushed away the captor's words with a wave of his hand." Yet he clearly demonstrated, even with this short effort, genuine storytelling ability.

That December, 1922, issue was doubly remarkable: for the emergence of Hammett with his first detective tale, and for "The False Burton Combs," a story by a thirty-three-year-old writer also relatively new to *Black Mask*, Carroll John Daly. (Having owned and operated the first film theater on the boardwalk in Atlantic City, Daly, working out of White Plains, New York, was now devoting himself to pulp fiction and had appeared once previously in the magazine two months earlier.) Written in the first person, "Combs" dealt with a nameless soldier of fortune: "I ain't a crook; just a gentleman adventurer and make my living against law breakers . . . I ain't a bird to fool with."

This no-name tough guy was the direct prototype for private detective Race Williams, created for *Black Mask* by Daly the following year. Williams gained instant acceptance among readers with his first case, "Knights of the Open Palm" (from the June 1, 1923 issue): "I'm what you might call a middleman—just a halfway house between the cops and the crooks . . . I do a little honest shooting once in a while—just in the way of business [but] I never bumped off a guy what didn't need it."

Race Williams was later described by his creator as age thirty, standing 5′ 11½″ and weighing in at 183, with dark brown hair and black eyes. "He admires a clever woman and respects a good one—when he finds her." Race was an

incredible marksman; in one story he fired from both of his big .45s simultaneously and a single hole appeared between the villain's eyes.

Williams was a loner, a tough-talking, rib-busting gent who took the law into his burly hands whenever he felt the police weren't getting there fast enough. During his violent career, Race gunned down several dozen assorted hoods and master villains ("You can't make hamburger without grinding up a little meat"), operating as a one-man death factory, yet avoiding all legal penalties.

Despite his popularity in the pulps, Daly was never a good writer. He created the hard-boiled, first-person-narrative private eye, but his style was crude, clumsy, unsubtle, his characters strictly one-dimensional. Daly knew nothing of crime and criminals, rarely ventured out of his home, loathed all outdoor sports. Race Williams was a fantasy creation (actually an extension of Daly's first *Black Mask* sleuth, Three-Gun Terry Mack), and for rival magazines, he later created Vee Brown, another cardboard detective.

Daly ended as he began, after three decades in the pulps, a man unable to rise above his material—and although his pioneering position in hard-boiled fiction cannot be disputed, it remained for Hammett's in-depth development and superior writing style to revolutionize the genre.

By mid-October of 1923, after three stories in *Black Mask* as "Collinson," Hammett, who had now abandoned the idea of writing poetry, finally appeared under his own name with a story called "Crooked Souls." (Although he had contributed letters under "S. D. Hammett," he dropped the Samuel when he began to write professional fiction.) This *Black Mask* tale, later reprinted as "The Gatewood Caper," featured a first person narrative by a nameless operative from the Continental Detective Agency in San Francisco, whose headquarters were "located in a

Market Street office building"—as were the headquarters of Pinkerton's in that city. In this same October 15 issue, Peter Collinson also had a story about the Continental Op, entitled "Slippery Fingers," which must surely have confused *Black Mask* readers. (This marked the last of the Collinson bylines.)

Actually, the Op made his debut—under the Collinson pen-name—in a tale published just two weeks earlier, "Arson Plus." In that one he described himself as "a busy, middle-aged detective" more interested in solving the crime than in "feminine beauty." From the outset, he was anti-women when it came to a case; the Op was all business. When he talked to a woman, "I discarded the trick stuff and came out cold-turkey." He'd been with Continental of San Francisco for "four or five years" and was an old hand at ducking bullets and reading truth behind lies. He was a hard customer, and readers took to him immediately, responding to the author's direct, no-nonsense approach to crime.

Dashiell Hammett's pre-Op work for *Black Mask* and *Brief Stories* lacked the bite of his Continental detective tales, though he dealt, in sardonic fashion, with the same "low-life" types encountered by the Op. Hammett would continue to produce occasional non-Op stories for *Black Mask,* but readers kept demanding new adventures starring the nameless little detective.

Hammett wrote to *Black Mask's* editor on the matter of the Op's lack of identity: "I didn't deliberately keep him nameless, but he got through 'Arson Plus' and 'Slippery Fingers' without needing a name, so I suppose I may as well let him run along that way. He's more or less of a type, and I'm not sure that he's entitled to a name. The private detective who is successful is neither the derby-hatted, broad-toed blockhead of one school of fiction, nor the all-knowing, infallible genius of another. I've worked with several of him. . . ."

Hammett had a very clear interior vision of the Op.

He had worked for a man he greatly respected in Pinkerton's Baltimore office, Assistant Superintendent James Wright—and over lunch at Luchow's Restaurant in New York many years later Hammett revealed that he'd modeled the Op directly on Wright. Of course, the Op was also Hammett; the crimes he solved and the crooks he met were often lifted directly out of the ex-detective's past. This lent an authenticity to Hammett's fiction which no other *Black Mask* contributor could match.

Over the next seven years, into 1930, Hammett would send the Op on a variety of realistic cases: he would be hired by insurance companies, businessmen, attorneys, housewives—always working out of the Continental agency in San Francisco, with the locale, in the majority of cases, being the city itself or the areas surrounding it. Mainly, Hammett sent him out to trace killers, investigate robberies, and to find missing or kidnapped persons, but the Op also functioned as guard, payoff man, house detective, and town-tamer.

The fat little detective disliked extravagant talk. "What's the use of getting poetic about it?" he'd snap at a client. "If you've got an honest job to be done, and want to pay an honest price for it, maybe I'll take it." And he was quick to fend off emotional females who wanted more from him than his services as a detective. "Well, good God, sister. I'm only a hired man with a hired man's interest in your troubles." (In later years, Raymond Chandler's Marlowe would echo these hard words to a teasing female who challenged his job. "I work at it, lady, I don't play at it.")

The second Op tale, "Slippery Fingers," was based on Hammett's knowledge of fingerprints, and when the editor questioned his method of faking them (Hammett's forger had coated the fingers with gelatin and pressed them into a copper plate etched with another man's prints) the author decisively replied: "The method used in my story was not selected because it is the best, but because it is the simplest with which I am acquainted and the most easily described.

Successful experiments were made with it by the experts at the Leavenworth federal prison."

Hammett created several continuing characters for the Op series. By his second case he had introduced associate Dick Foley as "the Agency's shadow ace," a character Hammett later described as "a swarthy little Canadian who stood nearly five feet in his high-heeled shoes, weighed a hundred pounds minus, talked like a Scotchman's telegram and could have shadowed a drop of salt water from the Golden Gate to Hongkong without ever losing sight of it." Also introduced on that second case was Bob Teal, "a youngster who will be a world-beater some day." (But he was short-lived; Hammett killed him off in a non-*Black Mask* tale late in 1924).

Dick Foley figured in a great many of the Op's adventures, as did Detective-Sergeant O'Gar, first mentioned in "Crooked Souls." O'Gar, "a squat man of fifty with sharp blue eyes," ran the Homicide Detail and always wore a black, wide-brimmed western sheriff's hat. Then there was "the Old Man," who gave the Op his orders, the taciturn white-mustached manager of the San Francisco Agency, in his seventies and "with no more warmth in him than a hangman's rope." Later, another agent, Mickey Linehan, was added to the series.

Although Hammett often described his Op as "heavy" or "thick-waisted," he made certain the reader would never doubt his character's basic hardness. "I'm no sensitive plant, and I've looked at a lot of unlovely sights in my time," says the Op on his fifth case, appropriately titled "Bodies Piled Up."

An editorial at the close of that year echoed the new author's acceptance. "Mr. Hammett has suddenly become one of the most popular of our *Black Mask* writers," proudly declared Sutton. "His stories are always entertaining, full of action, and very unusual situations."

Hammett's rising popularity was demonstrated early

in 1924, when he rated his first cover ("Featuring THE TENTH CLUE, an Amazing Detective Novelette by Dashiell Hammett") for his sixth Op adventure, the longest series effort at 10,000 words. This story was notable for a moody sequence in which the Op is slugged and dumped into the dark waters of San Francisco Bay. Moaning foghorns keep him awake in the icy water until he can be rescued. This sequence demonstrated Hammett's ability to utilize the area in dramatic terms; his streets, banks, offices were all quite real, all part of the San Francisco scene.

In the Thirties, Raymond Chandler utilized the Los Angeles area in similar fashion. The basic difference, however, is that Chandler allowed Philip Marlowe to describe his locale, to react to and record its beauty and ugliness, to remark at length on its physical characteristics, its flowers, trees, architecture. Hammett rarely did more than mention the name of a street or a building, in order to pinpoint his action. His San Francisco, undescribed, is therefore "timeless"—while Chandler's old Los Angeles, with its wooden oil derricks along La Brea and its bridle paths dividing Beverly Hills, no longer exists.

Under editor Sutton, Hammett published fourteen *Black Mask* tales (through March of 1924). Six of these were non-Op stories in which Hammett investigated various types of crime, including the compulsion to use a gun. The best was a western, "The Man Who Killed Dan Odams," in which Hammett handled the theme of a vengeance murder in stark, memorable terms. In another of the six, "The Second-Story Angel," he introduced a sweet-faced young girl crook who made fools out of several men, including the protagonist (who happened to be a crime writer). This story has special interest in that Hammett brought the girl, Angel Grace Cardigan, back for "The Big Knockover" and "$106,000 Blood Money" several years later.

During this same period Hammett sold another half-dozen stories to markets other than *Black Mask*. An interest-

ing character study, "The Green Elephant," was printed in H. L. Mencken's *Smart Set,* and featured a smalltime crook, Joe Shupe, "an unskilled laborer in the world of crime" who comes into accidental possession of a quarter of a million dollars. Emotionally unequipped to deal with this kind of "success," Joe all but cracks under the burden of such a treasure and is himself again only after he has been apprehended.

"Holiday," which appeared in *Pearson's* (July, 1923), was almost straight autobiography, detailing a tuberculosis patient's weekend across the border in Tijuana. Hammett later referred to it as "a nice but fairly pointless story about a lunger . . . going for a holiday from his hospital near San Diego." (The same one in which Hammett himself had been confined.) Until his unfinished autobiographical novel, *Tulip,* was written much later, it was the only piece of fiction Hammett produced which dealt with this nonviolent period of his life. The story is sensitively done, with full use of Hammett's eye for detail, and compares both in style and approach to Hemingway's autobiographical fiction about Nick Adams.

Writing to his editor, Sutton, about another of his non-Op efforts, "The Vicious Circle" (in which a blackmail victim has his tormentor murdered, only to face fresh blackmail from the hired killer), Hammett discussed the story's background and characters: "In the years during which I tried my hand at private detecting I ran across several cases where the 'friend' called in to dispose of a blackmailer either went into partnership with him or took over his game after getting him out of the way."

By April of 1924, *Black Mask* had a new editor, Phil Cody, while valuable Harry North stayed on as his assistant. Cody and North sensibly concentrated on headlining Hammett, Carroll John Daly, and Erle Stanley Gardner. (The creator of the famed Perry Mason novels was just beginning his long writing career; as "Charles M. Green"

Gardner had made his first *Black Mask* appearance just four months before with a wildly melodramatic scare-tale, "The Shrieking Skeleton.")

"Cody had a keen appreciation of literature and of the detective story," Gardner later stated. "With Cody, the action type of detective story took a long stride forward."

Under his new editor, Hammett published what might be termed his first two-part serial, in that "The House in Turk Street" was directly related to its sequel, "The Girl With the Silver Eyes." The two Op stories totaled nearly 24,000 words, and brought their author much closer to the novel form.

Hammett occasionally repeated his effects: he was particularly fond of shootouts in darkened rooms and of young, helpless girls being pursued through midnight streets. A favorite Hammett theme was cross-treachery, in which an amoral band of crooks would play off against one another for individual gain. His central character in this type of story was a woman, beautiful, soft-eyed, self-seeking, who would not hesitate to pile one lie upon another in order to convince, who would use her sex as a weapon, her charm as a shield, who was wholly without scruples. Such a girl was red-haired Elvira from "The House in Turk Street," a direct prototype of *The Maltese Falcon's* Brigid O'Shaughnessy. ("A white face between a bobbed mass of flame-colored hair. Smoke-gray eyes that were set too far apart for trustworthiness—though not for beauty . . . her red mouth laughed at me, exposing the edges of little sharp animal teeth. She was as beautiful as the devil, and twice as dangerous.")

It is interesting to trace the roots of the *Falcon* in these two related stories. Tai, the fat Chinese gang leader with the oily tongue is an early Casper Gutman—and the trigger-happy Hook offers a preview of the gun-toting Wilmer from *Falcon*. The Op plays Sam Spade's role in dealing with them, some hidden bonds serving in place of the

jeweled Black Bird. The Op has the bonds, but the fat man has him—as Gutman had Spade who had the bird. Hammett was not yet able to develop these characters with the mature brilliance he evidenced in *Falcon,* but their roots are clearly here. In the sequel story, "The Girl With the Silver Eyes," we have a preview scene of Brigid's attempt to seduce Spade into freeing her, as Elvira, captured by the Op, spins her lying story in the hope of release. She loses. The implacable Op turns her in to pay for the lives of the men she destroyed. Truth wins over beauty.

An oddity: Hammett tells us here that the Op is thirty-five; in later stories he reaches forty and remains so. Apparently Hammett then considered a man in his mid-thirties as being middle-aged, though he himself was only six years younger.

As he often did during this period, Hammett wrote a letter to the editor concerning his story. (This was a regular *Black Mask* feature for many years. An author would discuss his story under the heading: "From the Author of——.") Hammett admitted that "most of the details [of "The Girl With the Silver Eyes"] are based on things I've either run into personally or heard second hand from other detectives. Joplin's roadhouse . . . is exactly as I have set it down. And stoolie Porky Grout's original died of tuberculosis in Butte, Montana, three years ago. . . . Stool pigeons are almost without exception more cowardly even than the ordinary crook, yet they follow the most dangerous calling in the criminal world. Not only is their world against them, but the detectives who use them seldom hesitate to sacrifice them if anything is gained thereby."

In August, 1924, *Black Mask* readers were jolted: two Hammett Op stories had been rejected, and the magazine was bragging about it! Cody and North had tightened the editorial reins, and were returning manuscripts which they felt needed additional work. In a letter to Harry North, Hammett agreed firmly with their position: "The trouble

is, this sleuth of mine has degenerated into a meal ticket. . . . and recently I've fallen into the habit of bringing him out and running him around whenever the landlord, or the butcher, or the grocer shows signs of nervousness. . . . There are men who can write like that, but I am not one of them. If I stick to the stuff I want to write . . . I can make a go of it, but when I try to grind out a yarn because I think there's a market for it, then I flop. . . . I have a liking for honest work and honest work, as I see it, is work that is done for the worker's enjoyment as much as for the profit it will bring him . . . so, whenever I get hold of a story that fits my sleuth I shall put him to work, but I'm through trying to run him on a schedule . . . I want to thank you and Mr. Cody for jolting me into wakefulness. There's no telling how much good this will do me."

Hammett revised one of the two rejected manuscripts, "Women, Politics and Murder," and it was printed later that year, a story notable for the Op's hardening attitude toward violence: "I began to throw my right fist into him. I liked that. His belly was flabby, and it got softer every time I hit it. I hit it often."

At this stage in his career, Hammett was in severe financial trouble. The low-paying penny-a-word pulps were not supporting him, and his salary at the jewelry store was meager. His bohemian existence—a girl across the hall on Pine Street, another on Grant, red wine on the table, and loud writer-talk from fellow pulpists—was good only on the surface. He was still fighting the lung disease; he ate cheap food or no food at all; he worked all night at his typewriter, living on coffee, soup and cigarettes, unwashed dishes strewn about the kitchen, the fog-damp cold around him.

But he would keep his promise to Harry North.

He would write only one way: the best he knew how.

4

FROM CODY TO "CAP" SHAW

By the close of 1924 violence and corruption ruled America. Leopold and Loeb had butchered Bobby Franks; a senator from Vermont was severely wounded in the nation's capital by a stray bullet fired during an open-street Washington gun battle between Prohibition agents and bootleggers; in baseball, the coach of the Giants tried to buy off a Philadelphia shortstop and was convicted in a pennant scandal; a Negro was beaten to death for swearing at his employer in Texas; Dion O'Banion had been gunned down in his own flower shop in Chicago, a city rocked by bomb and bullet as Capone and Johnny Torrio and Bugs Moran and other bigtime mobsters battled for control, aided by such notables as Hymie Weiss and Three-Gun Alterie. That was the season they put away Celia Cooney, "the bobbed-hair bandit," for twenty years. A Chicago reporter declared: "We are living by the code of the Dark Ages."

Hammett, of course, was well aware of all this. From his vantage point in the wide-open city of San Francisco, he saw graft operating at every level of the political and business worlds. This "climate of corruption" was reflected in his fiction.

A December issue of *Argosy All-Story* published Hammett's novelet, "Nightmare Town." This tale, a direct forerunner of the "Poisonville" *(Red Harvest)* series, treats the same theme of total corruption—as Hammett sketches a

town wholly owned by thieves and murderers which hero Steve Threefall enters against his will. The place is called Izzard, located on the Nevada-California line. In the course of the narrative Steve links up with heroine Nova Vallance; at the climax, with half the town after them, they head for Izzard's one honest soul, Blind Rymer. Yet that sweet old gentleman hauls out a brace of pistols and reveals himself to be as crooked as all the other townspeople. Armed only with an ebony walking stick, Steve escapes with the girl, but they must fight their way clear. In that final, wild tour de force of a climax Hammett creates total action on the printed page: "Men filled the doorway. A gun roared and a piece of the ceiling flaked down. Steve . . . charged the door . . . the stick whipped backward and forward and . . . the rhythm of incessant thudding against flesh and clicking on bone became a tune that sang through the grunts of fighting men. . . . [Outside, at the car] Steve threw himself forward, swinging his stick against shin and thigh, toppling men from the machine. With his left hand he swept the girl to his side. His body shook and rocked under the weight of blows. . . . He swung the girl over the door, hammered her down . . . upon the legs of a man . . . heard bone break. . . . The machine began to move. Holding on with his hands, he lashed both feet out behind . . . then struck stiff-fingered into a broad red face . . . a man fell on the girl. Steve pulled him off—tore pieces from him—tore hair and flesh. The car swerved, scraped a building, scraped one side clear of men. . . . Steve fell into the seat beside the girl. . . . Pistols exploded behind them . . . a bitter-voiced rifle emptied itself at them . . . and then the desert—white and smooth as a gigantic hospital bed—was around them."

As the wicked town burns behind them, a Biblical Sodom and Gomorrah, Steve and Nova drive off, Steve thinking, "What a fight! What a fight!"

Another strong story of this period, "Ruffian's Wife" (from *Sunset*), marked a departure for Hammett, in that he wrote the story in a subjective, third person style, from the

viewpoint of a woman, the wife of "ruffian" Guy Tharp. The toughness of the legendary Tharp is shaken by the threat of a perfumed fat man, Leonidas Doucas (another early prototype for Casper Gutman of *Falcon*). Doucas is eventually killed by Tharp, but with his wife's help. In saving her brutal husband, she surrenders the idealistic image she had built; reality has replaced fantasy in her life. "Ruffian's Wife" is extremely well written, a fictional experiment which Hammett brought off quite successfully.

He was now very close to full maturity in his development of the action-character story, and over a nine-month period (March through December, 1925) he produced five superb Continental Op novelets in a row for *Black Mask*. These stories, totaling some 92,000 words, demonstrate his unique ability to build solid characterizations within a framework of action and deductive logic. By 1926, with full justification, editor Cody was billing Hammett as "a master of the craft."

The first of the five novelets, "The Whosis Kid," offers another brief preview-glimpse of a *Maltese Falcon* character. The Kid, Hammett later admitted, formed the tryout basis for *Falcon's* homosexual boy-gunman, Wilmer.

"The Scorched Face," second of the five, embraces a "cult" in a foreshadowing of *The Dain Curse*. Here much of the action is presented in short, jolting paragraphs:

> A body came out of nowhere, hit my back, flattened me to the landing.
>
> The feel of silk. . . . A brawny hand was fumbling at my throat.
>
> I bent my wrist until my gun, upside down, lay against my cheek. Praying for my ear, I squeezed.
>
> My cheek took fire. . . .
>
> The silk slid away.
>
> Paul hauled me upright.
>
> We started down the stairs.

With "Corkscrew," Hammett got the Op out of San Francisco. He sent him to the town in Arizona for which the story is named, fitted him out with cowboy clothes, a fast-stepping horse, and a pair of sixguns, and involved him with such rough hombres as Gyp Rainey, Milk River, and various Circle H.A.R. ranch riders. The Op drank at Bardell's Border Palace, brawled with the town bully, tamed a bucking bronc and dry-gulched villains. None of which surprised *Black Mask* readers in 1925. The magazine regularly published western fiction, and more often than not the cover would feature an old-West action painting. (Erle Stanley Gardner wrote several sagebrush sagas, starring gunslinger Black Barr.) In "Corkscrew" Hammett was having some fun with his Op, and the story—though not typical of Hammett's usual crime work—is one of his best.

Actually, as Philip Durham and other critics have observed, the private detective is a direct carry-over from the western gunman, the folk hero of legend, who righted wrongs with a weapon at his hip, who preserved the ideals of justice and truth against a background of violence. The old and new West blended in the image of the private detective.

Hammett's next novelet, "Dead Yellow Women," was set in San Francisco's colorful, mysterious Chinatown, a world as dangerous as Izzard, the "nightmare town." In a carefully-structured, brilliantly-realized story, Hammett created one of his most memorable characters, the effusive, snake-treacherous Chang Li Ching who addresses the fat little Op as, variously, "the Father of Detectives, the Prince of Thief-Catchers, the Emperor of Hawkshaws, the Unveiler of Secrets, the Terror of Evildoers, the Lord of Snares, the King of Finders-Out." The Op is unruffled; he knows he must never turn his back on Chang. Their head-on meetings are written with immense zest.

Hammett knew Chinatown, and once recounted the tale of being offered a Chinese muscle-man. "In those days

if you ran a joint you had a bodyguard whether you needed one or not, just to rate. There was this roly-poly Chinese pansy offered to me by a friend who owned a dive down there, to use if I had anybody I wanted pushed around—a leg broken or something—but I wasn't to spoil him by giving him money for this service. 'Five or ten bucks is okay for a tip,' I was told, but no more. I didn't take advantage of the offer—but I *did* write the Chinese into a picture much later in Hollywood."

The final story in Hammett's 1925 output has since become one of his most frequently reprinted efforts, "The Gutting of Couffignal." The action takes place on an imaginary island in San Pablo Bay. Like "Corkscrew" and "Dead Yellow Women," it is an extravaganza, a wildly violent example of Hammett at full throttle. The climactic scene, between the Op and the tricky Princess Zhukovski, offered Hammett a final rehearsal before he was to pit Spade against Brigid for their memorable *Falcon* showdown. "I'm a detective because I happen to like the work," says the Op. "And liking work makes you want to do it as well as you can. . . . That's the fix I'm in . . . catching crooks is the only kind of sport I know anything about. . . . You think I'm a man and you're a woman. That's wrong. I'm a manhunter and you're something that has been running in front of me. There's nothing human about it. . . ."

When she tries to get away he shoots her in the leg.

Hammett's eight-year struggle with tuberculosis ended in 1925; he was pronounced fully cured of the lung ailment, a cause for personal celebration. He had his wife and daughter rejoin him in San Francisco. Before a year had passed a second daughter would be born to the Hammetts. Now, with a family to support, the bills increased, and his writing time was cut severely. Although he sold *Black Mask* three more stories (all of which appeared early in 1926), he could not keep up the pace. For almost a full year no Hammett fiction was printed.

Two of these 1926 stories are worth examining, since

they introduced a pair of new Hammett detectives: Robin Thin, from "The Nails in Mr. Cayterer," and Alec Rush, from "The Assistant Murderer." No two detectives could be further removed in character. Thin, who worked for his father, was a young would-be poet, a reluctant manhunter who would rather pursue verse than criminals. His first-person narrative is flowery and self-conscious, and in his weakness and affectations Robin Thin remains one of Hammett's least convincing creations. (A second of the poet-detective's cases, "The Figure of Incongruity," was written during this period, but the magazine it sold to failed to appear, and the story did not reach print until 1961, when it was published by *Ellery Queen's Mystery Magazine* under the title, "A Man Named Thin.")

Hammett's other 1926 detective, derby-hatted, cigar-smoking Alec Rush, was described as "fat, grizzled, battered and ugly . . . with savage red eyes." He worked out of a seedy office in Hammett's home town of Baltimore. An ex-cop, he had been "chucked out of the department," but had avoided corruption. "Can I buy you, Rush?" asks the killer. And the ugly detective says, "No . . . don't let my looks and record kid you." (A philosophy Sam Spade is to echo three years later when he tells Brigid, "Don't be too sure I'm as crooked as I'm supposed to be.")

Hammett may have intended using Rush in other stories, but no sequel appeared.

Having moved to 620 Eddy Street, a four-story apartment dwelling built shortly after the quake, Hammett listed himself (in a local census) as "advertising manager for A.S. Samuels," and made no mention of being a writer. He was now doing layout work as well as copywriting for Samuels, and had been given an office on the second floor, with an assistant, Peggy O'Toole. Miss O'Toole had no idea, as she worked with Hammett, that she would eventually appear, in fictional form, as Brigid O'Shaughnessy in *The Maltese Falcon.*

The editor who would encourage Hammett in the

creation of this classic novel came to *Black Mask* in November of 1926. Phil Cody, who had edited the magazine for two and a half years, was replaced by Joseph Thompson Shaw. (The publication's official pre-Shaw title was *The Black Mask,* but with his first issue Shaw shortened it to *Black Mask.*)

"Cap" Shaw, as he was called, was fifty-two, a graduate of Bowdoin College, where he had won the national championship in sabers. During the First World War he had been a captain in charge of bayonet instruction, and had served for five years as chief of a Hoover mission in Czechoslovakia. He had never seen or heard of *Black Mask* before being asked to edit it, nor did he have any knowledge of pulp fiction.

However, he was determined, from the day he sat behind the editor's desk, to make *Black Mask* a magazine to remember.

Cody had been a fine editor, but Shaw would be a finer one; his pride and soldier's stubbornness would see to that. First, he would give the magazine a unified aspect by using only one interior artist: Arthur Rodman Bowker. Second, he would cull any weak fiction from the inventory. This decision resulted in the rejection of a new Dashiell Hammett story. The author was furious at Shaw's abrupt turndown. He was through with *Black Mask,* and told Shaw precisely that. (Which pleased Eltinge Warner, the president of *Black Mask's* Pro-Distributors Publishing Company, who did not like Hammett's work.)

Shaw, however, was upset. He didn't want to see Hammett leave the magazine, and talked over the problem with Erle Stanley Gardner, who wrote to his fellow author, urging him to reconsider.

Shaw also wrote Hammett a letter, explaining his extensive plans to upgrade *Black Mask.* Shaw made suggestions on expanding the Op, and asked Hammett to send in a novel if possible. He got an immediate reply. "You've hit

on exactly what I've been thinking about and working toward," Hammett stated. "As I see it, the approach I have in mind has never been attempted. The field is unscratched and wide open."

The lamb was back in the fold.

Shaw never took credit for having "discovered" the big names in *Black Mask*: Hammett, Daly, Gardner, Raoul Whitfield, Frederick Nebel, Nels Jorgenson, Tom Curry, and others—though one of the greatest of "the *Black Mask* boys," Raymond Chandler, sold his first story to Shaw in 1933. ("All I did was buy it; Chandler had done all the work, and the skill and talent existed on paper from his first page!")

Authentic adventure was Shaw's requirement, and he leaned toward writers who were themselves men of action. He boasted of Hammett's Pinkerton years; Tom Curry was an ex-police reporter; Whitfield had been a World War I flier and had bummed through China and the Philippines; Gardner was a world traveler, treasure hunter, and sportsman; Nels Leroy Jorgenson was a New Jersey motorcycle cop; Horace McCoy, soon to join their ranks, had been a fighter pilot in Europe. It must have warmed Shaw's heart when slight, card-playing, unadventurous Carroll John Daly (who wouldn't fix his teeth due to a fear of dentists) was arrested for carrying a concealed weapon; he was found packing a big Race Williams-type .45 in his belt!

It was said that Shaw himself, as a crack fencer, had perfected a thrust with the épée against which there was no known defensive stroke. (Shaw published several books, some detective novels among them, one of which bore the colorfully tough title, *Blood on the Curb*.)

Cap knew what he wanted at *Black Mask*, and he selected Hammett as the trail-blazer, the man who could set the pace. "Hammett was the leader in the thought that finally brought the magazine its distinctive form," Shaw later declared. "I wanted to make full use of his rare ability

of observation and his gift to analyze character beneath a surface appearance. . . . Hammett told his stories with a new kind of compulsion and authenticity. . . . We wanted action, but action is meaningless unless it involves recognizable human character in three-dimensional form. It was on this concept that we began to shape the magazine."

When a new challenger enters the arena, it is necessary that he defeat the ruling champion. Manolete had to be met and destroyed in the bullring before the young Dominguin could become Spain's *El Numero Uno*. Hammett was about to write his first novel, and the reigning detective novelist in America was Willard Huntington Wright, known to countless readers, librarians, and booksellers as S.S. Van Dine. Van Dine's suave detective, Philo Vance, had earned a fortune for the exotic, bearded man who created him.

In mid-January of 1927, challenger met champ in open print, as Hammett published a lethal review of Van Dine's latest, *The Benson Murder Case*, in the *The Saturday Review of Literature*: "The murderer's identity becomes obvious quite early in the story. The authorities, no matter how stupid the author chose to make them, would have cleared up the mystery promptly if they had been allowed to follow the most rudimentary police routine. . . . Vance is a bore when he discusses art and philosophy . . . his conversational manner is that of a high-school girl who has been studying the foreign words and phrases in the back of her dictionary . . . and he manages always, and usually ridiculously, to be wrong. . . . The author . . . doesn't let his policemen ask any questions that aren't wholly irrelevant. . . . Their fingerprint experts are excluded from the scene of the crime . . . and when information concerning a mysterious box of jewelry accidentally bobs up everybody resolutely ignores it, since it would have led to a solution before the three-hundredth page. . . . Mr. Van Dine doesn't deprive his officials of every liberty, however: he generously lets

them compete with Vance . . . in the expression of idiocies."

(In 1944, Raymond Chandler was to agree with Hammett on Vance, referring to Wright's detective as "probably the most asinine character in American fiction.")

Hammett was certain that his brand of hard-boiled impact fiction would replace the outmoded crime writing of the Van Dine school. But he still had to prove himself to the reading public, and his emergence as a published novelist was two years away.

The first Hammett "novel" was less than 40,000 words in length—made up of two linked adventures, "The Big Knockover" and "$106,000 Blood Money." Released in book form much later as *Blood Money*, it starred the redoubtable Op and began with a spectacular holdup of two major San Francisco banks. Here was the most extensive Op saga Hammett had yet attempted.

In announcing "The Big Knockover," editor Shaw tried to forestall any criticism regarding the tale's "super-crime" aspects: "Before they actually do it, one is inclined to say it isn't done. But the gang warfare in Illinois, the big mail-truck holdup in Jersey, found bandits using airplanes, bombs, and machine guns—and now Mr. Hammett pictures a daring action that is . . . stunning in its scope . . . yet can anyone be sure it isn't likely to occur?"

The action was indeed stunning: more than 150 gangsters, gathered from around the nation, descended on the Seaman's National and the Golden Gate Trust. In the double robbery, sixteen policemen died along with a dozen spectators. Seven of the bandits were gunned to death, others speeding off in various directions. Yet the bloodletting had just begun; as the Op got into the case he found that the gangs were mowing each other down over the loot. He finds fourteen dead crooks on Fillmore, hits another house to find six more bodies. The roll call on the dead reveals Hammett at his most inventive: "There was the Dis-and-Dat Kid, who crashed out of Leavenworth only

two months before . . . L.A. Slim, from Denver, sockless as usual, with a thousand-dollar bill sewed in each shoulder of his coat; Spider Girrucci, wearing a steel-mesh vest under his shirt and a scar from crown to chin . . . Bull McGonickle, still pale from fifteen years in Joliet; Toby the Lugs, who used to brag about picking President Wilson's pocket in a Washington vaudeville theatre . . . Donkey Marr, last of the bow-legged Marrs, killers all, father and five sons; Toots Salda . . . who had once picked up and run away with two Savannah coppers . . . and Rumdum Smith, who killed Lefty Read in Chi—a rosary wrapped around his left wrist."

In "The Big Knockover" the Op is an animalistic man of violence, pain-prone; a fight tones his system, fires his blood: "My blackjack crunched the arm of the man in front. . . . I trusted my arms and legs and saved bullets. . . . It was a swell bag of nails. Swing right, swing left, kick, swing right, swing left, kick. Don't hesitate, don't look for targets. God will see to it there's always a mug for your gun or blackjack to sock, a belly for your foot. . . ."

And later: "I was . . . wondering if I was now enjoying the rewards of my virtue—in a heaven where I could enjoy myself forever . . . socking folks who had been rough with me."

In a sweep of headlong action, the Op punches and shoots his way through the narrative, wrapping things up by nailing Bluepoint Vance and Big Flora, both in on the caper. But he allows the "mastermind" to escape, a string-thin old Greek named Papadopoulos who takes the girl in the case, Nancy Regan, with him on the runout. The Op vows to get him—which leads into the sequel.

Published in *Black Mask* three months later, "$106,000 Blood Money" (a title referring to the reward offered) maintained the pace of the first story, with the Op surviving an ambush set up by a young man he trusted, Jack Counihan, a fellow operative out of Continental. At the climax, we learn that Counihan had fallen for Nancy and "gone

bad" under her influence. The disgraced young Op is shot to death, and the veteran reports it all to the Old Man. Both the Old Man and the Op are relieved that Jack's death will seem heroic to the press; the Agency will not get "a black eye." The Op says he wants a couple of weeks off, that he's "tired, washed out." The novel ends on this gray note of exhaustion.

There are too many gratuitous killings, too much melodramatic action piled on action for Hammett to develop the depth of character required for a successful novel, yet this two-parter displays masterful pacing and a tremendous zest for narrative and situation. Philip Durham stated: "If there is such a thing as the poetry of violence, Hammett clearly achieved it in this first novel . . . hero, style and setting had developed beyond the limits of the short story."

Critic Richard Schickel finds, in this early Hammett, the seeds of "the modern existential anti-hero," describing the Op as "job-oriented, stirred only by the most brutal sensationalism (the chase, physical danger, armed combat), either incapable of or totally uninterested in normal social (or sexual) intercourse, showing no emotion except, at the end, a total revulsion with human nature as it has been revealed to him."

This "total revulsion" would reach its zenith in Hammett's next major effort, a novel destined to send a shock wave through literature when it appeared in book form.

5

A HARVEST AND A CURSE

By october, 1927, joseph shaw was able to announce to his readers a new series "by the foremost writer of action-detective fiction in America." In November the first section of *Red Harvest* appeared as "The Cleansing of Poisonville," which Shaw carefully pointed out as "not a serial, but a series of four complete adventures . . . [dealing] with a city whose administrators have gone mad with power and lust of wealth. It is, to our minds, the ideal detective story—the new type of fiction which *Black Mask* is seeking to develop."

Poet Robert Graves later called this novel "an acknowledged literary landmark." Its locale is the imaginary mining town of Personville (nicknamed "Poisonville" by those who know it), situated near Ogden, Utah, and controlled by various gangster factions held in delicate and tenuous check by mutual respect and fear. The Op arrives on a call from the publisher of the local paper, Don Willsson, a civic reformer. Willsson is shot to death that same night, and the Op goes to his father, old Elihu Willsson, who owns most of the city, working with ganglords Pete the Finn, Lew Yard, Max "Whisper" Thayler, and Noonan, the corrupt police chief. Elihu, having seen his son gunned down, fearful for his life, hires the Op to "clean up Poisonville."

The Op accepts the job, shrewdly and coldly deciding to play off one gangster against another. He accompanies Chief Noonan on a raid against "Whisper's place," but ducks inside to warn Whisper that Noonan is out to get him, thus setting off a chain of killings, dynamitings, and shootouts.

Shaw was delighted with reader response to the bloody saga, editorially commenting: "We are hearing about this Poisonville series from all over the country."

From chapter to chapter, the Op uses his veteran's knowledge of human weakness to drain the poison from Poisonville. Although he drinks with the town's brassy playgirl, Dinah Brand, he does not make love to her; such entanglements leave a detective open to attack; the Op wants no flaws in his armor.

Red Harvest has been termed allegorical, in that the detective, according to critic Robert Edenbaum, "has become godlike in his immunity from temptation . . . a manipulator . . . who experiments with the forces that move human beings to destruction."

As Dante used his native Florence as a model for hell, as Dickens depicted the horrors of London with its lust, poverty and crime, as Melville projected his gothic vision of New York as "an inferno into which the hero falls"—so Hammett utilized Poisonville.

In each Hammett episode the "red harvest" mounts; by the last of the series more than thirty deaths are toted up, a total which includes twelve of the nineteen main characters. Whisper is gone. So is Dinah Brand and Noonan and Yard and Pete and Finn and Reno Starkey, another major hood.

As it was, Hammett had toned down the magazine version when he reworked it as his first published book; he removed several dynamitings and shootings, yet it remained amazingly violent, so much so that André Gide called *Red Harvest* "the last word in atrocity, cynicism, and

horror." Gide also credited Hammett for "a remarkable achievement" and rated the dialogue "with the best in Hemingway."

A review in *The Bookman* echoed this comparison: "It is doubtful if even Ernest Hemingway has ever written more effective dialogue than may be found within the pages of this extraordinary tale. . . . [Hammett's] characters speak the crisp, hard-boiled language of the underworld."

The Fatima-smoking, poker-playing Op was forty in this novel, a man battered by life, hitherto impervious to death. Yet even he almost cracks in the course of the bloody events in Poisonville. (In a revised section, written for the book version, the Op tells us: "I've got hard skin over what's left of my soul, and after twenty years of messing around with crime I can look at any sort of murder without seeing anything in it but my bread and butter . . . but this getting a rear out of planning deaths is not natural to me. It's what this place has done to me.")

The Op has become uncertain in his role as mass executioner. Early in the action he had declared: "Poisonville is ripe for the harvest. It's a job I like, and I'm going to do it." But the job turns sour; the hard-souled detective sees too much death. "This burg's getting me," he says. "If I don't get away soon I'll be going blood-simple like the natives." He finishes and gets out.

With Hammett's detectives, it was always the job that mattered, the job assigned, the job that had to be done against lawbreakers—the small, near-futile but *necessary* acts that shored the crumbling banks of society against the tides of corruption. Hammett and his Op were basically cynical; they felt things wouldn't really change (". . . you'll have your city back, all nice and clean and ready to go to the dogs again") but someone had to do something, and that was the Op's job. He was that someone.

On a technical level, *Red Harvest* reflects Hammett's careful approach to the novel form, his attention to the

smallest detail in dialogue and description. Comparing the magazine segments against the book, one finds, as with all of Hammett's major novels from *Black Mask,* a reworking process that covers the entire story, page by page. A "You're mistaken, my dear" becomes simply: "Wrong." The magazine's ". . . and ran out to follow my advice" is changed to the more direct ". . . and went away." Again, a "Who for?" takes the place of a stilted "For whom?" Also, like F. Scott Fitzgerald, Hammett would sometimes "cannibalize" sections of early magazine stories for his books. He lifted a description of the Agency's Old Man directly out of "The Big Knockover" and inserted it in the book version of *Red Harvest.* (Hammett never intended that any of his early magazine work be printed in book form; he agreed to it, years later, only after strong urging from publishers and agents. This accounts for the same "Old Man" section from *Red Harvest* turning up in the later-published *Blood Money.*)

In *Red Harvest,* Hammett was endlessly inventive in his method of reporting gunfire:

> . . . a dozen guns emptied themselves . . .
>
> . . . a bullet kissed a hole in the door frame . . .
>
> . . . an automobile came down the street toward me, moving fast, leaking gunfire from the rear . . .
>
> . . . the machine-gun settled down to business, grinding out metal like the busy little death factory it was . . .
>
> . . . bullets bit chunks out of the car's curtains . . .
>
> . . . slugs were cutting at us from a wooden building . . .
>
> . . . a gun said something, the same thing four times, roaring like a 16-inch rifle under the iron roof . . .

Writing for *The Saturday Review,* Ben Ray Redman later observed: "With *Red Harvest,* the hard-boiled school of detective fiction, bound in hard covers, moved out from the back room of the pulps into the bright light of the best

bookstores. The private eye was stepping forward to claim his kingdom."

Critic Martin Maloney found the Conan Doyle image completely shattered: "It is a long step from Holmes pondering the significance of a flake of cigar ash . . . to Hammett's Op, who, on one occasion, stuffs a length of copper wire into his pocket because it's just the right length to go around somebody's neck. The verb 'to pursue' now becomes . . . 'to destroy' . . . and the black-and-white universe of Holmes vanishes. . . .The burden of guilt for crime tends to spread, so that no one is free of it."

Hammett's next major effort, *The Dain Curse,* was the third and final novel to feature the Continental Op (and only three more Op stories would appear in *Black Mask*—through 1930—before Hammett permanently retired his fat little sleuth).

In many ways the most complex of Hammett's novels, this four-part history of "the Black Dains" is notable for its dazzling invention, intricate cross-plotting and multiple climaxes. On the surface, the plot lends itself to parody, and crime specialist John Bartlow Martin (in *Harper's Magazine*) found the story wildly overdone: "In this single Hammett novel the detective shot and stabbed one man to death, helped shoot another dead, was himself attacked with dagger, gun, chloroform and bomb, fought off a ghostly manifestation barehanded, wrestled with five women, cured a girl of narcotic addiction—and . . . was obliged to deal with one seduction, eight murders, a jewel burglary, and a family curse."

The book, which incidentally dealt with diamonds, was dedicated to Albert S. Samuels, the San Francisco jeweler who had employed Hammett. (The author was paying a debt, as he did in dedicating *Red Harvest* to Joseph T. Shaw.) Actually, Hammett had borrowed more than a working knowledge of diamond-cutting from his job with

Samuels, since several characters in *The Dain Curse* were named after store employees.

"Leggett was our switchboard operator," says Samuels. "David Riese, who also worked for us, became a doctor in the novel—and a minor character was named after our Mrs. Priestly, who was in silverware."

Although Hammett was soon earning enough money from his books to enable him to leave Samuels for good, he kept in touch with the jeweler over the years—and Samuels recalls the time he became very ill in San Francisco. Hammett found out about the illness, and immediately offered his old employer personal aid.

"He was an important screen writer down in Hollywood by then," Samuels states, "but when he heard I was bad off he came right up to see me—all the way from Los Angeles in a chauffeur-driven Rolls!"

The Dain Curse (written for *Black Mask* as separate novelets to please Shaw, who disliked using serials) suffers in its adaptation to book form. Lacking the cohesive element of a single locale, this story jumps from seacoast to city to country, while the reader is forced to cope with over thirty characters (including Eric Collinson, in which Hammett paid tongue-in-cheek tribute to his old pen name). That he could bring the story off at all is to his credit—and there are few writers who could have unified the narrative's disparate parts as well as he—yet to some extent one could agree with Hammett himself who later called it "a silly story." *The Dain Curse* marked a plateau, not an upward step, in his career.

However, this novel had many admirers—among them Ernest Hemingway, who (in his *Death in the Afternoon*) publicly revealed himself as a Hammett fan. "My eyes were too bad to read," stated Hemingway, who was then suffering temporary eye trouble in Spain, "and my wife was reading Dashiell Hammett's bloodiest to date, *The Dain Curse*,

out loud. . . ." Apparently, if Hemingway could not read Hammett he wanted Hammett read to him.

Threading her way through this complex story was a young girl Hammett called Gabrielle Leggett, who bore "the terrible curse" of the Dain family. In contrast to the female villains Hammett was fond of portraying, Gabrielle was victim rather than aggressor, pursued by many men who were destroyed in seeking her love, a girl who turns to morphine in an effort to escape a dark reality, and who is eventually cured by the Op. Hammett came closer to allowing his detective to love a woman in this relationship than in any previous Op story. "Let yourself go," the detective soothes her in the midst of the harrowing cure. "I'll take care of you."

She asks the Op how he could have put up with her. Why did he do it? "I'm damned if I'll make a chump of myself by telling you why I did it, why it was neither revolting or disgusting, why I'd do it again and be glad of the chance."

She takes this as a declaration of his love—but he quickly covers ("I don't mean anything that I'll admit"). The Op tells her he's "an old man" and speaks of another woman—but his tone reveals the girl has come close to piercing his emotional armor.

The girl's mother, father, husband, stepmother, doctor and "religious counselor" all die during the story, but the Op breaks the "black curse" and Gabrielle is allowed to live, to find happiness: the knight has dissolved the magic spell and set the maiden free. Now he can ride on to the next castle; more dragons await the sword; but his escape has been a narrow one. He learns that it is easier to turn an evil woman over to the law than to walk away from a good one.

This darkly fanciful fairy tale aura of good-versus-evil permeates *The Dain Curse,* and there is a splendidly chilling scene in which the Op, half-drugged with chloroform,

must battle what seems to him a ghost, yet a ghost with substance which bleeds as he lashes at it: " . . . the thing squirmed and writhed, shuddered and shivered, swirling wildly now, breaking apart, reuniting madly in the black air. . . ." The blood is his own, the Op discovers, breaking free into unpolluted air. Yet no sooner is he clear of this "ghost" than he is forced to use his gun against a knife-wielding fanatic, Joseph Haldorn, who considers himself God. The Op is badly shaken by a seemingly supernatural defense against bullets: "I fired. The bullet hit his cheek. I saw the hole it made. No muscle twitched . . . not even his eyes blinked. He walked deliberately, not hurrying, towards me. I worked the automatic's trigger, pumping six more bullets [in the magazine version it was *seven*] into his face and body. I saw them go in. And he came on steadily, showing in no way that he was conscious of them. . . . The knife in his hand went up high above his head . . . he was bringing retribution to me." The Op, too, has a knife—a dagger—and now he uses it. "I drove the blade into his throat, in till the hilt's cross stopped it. Then I was through."

This does it. Joseph falls, and the Op sighs, "Thank God he wasn't really God." The cross—the dagger—has killed the demon; the knight has triumphed over evil.

The four segment titles convey the flavor of the story: "Black Lives," "The Hollow Temple," "Black Honeymoon," "Black Riddle."

Philip Durham finds in *The Dain Curse* that the Op has "grown old and soft," claiming that Hammett "traded a hard-boiled hero for a part-time sentimentalist." This is only partially true, since Hammett actually added depth to the Op's character by allowing him to become more sensitive. But Hammett did "soften" the little detective when he revised the series for hard-cover publication, deleting a scene in which the Op uses his pistol to kill a certain Mrs. Fink. (Actually, by rough count, the Op personally

killed no less than fifteen men and women in line of duty during the course of his seven-year *Black Mask* career, wounding at least another dozen or so.)

A lengthy sequence in the magazine version involved a seedy dwelling, The Primrose Hotel, run by a former tent showman, Felix Weber (who'd once drunkenly fired a .45 slug at the Op). This sequence was dropped when the story reached hard covers; Hammett turned the Primrose into the Temple of the Holy Grail, with Joseph Haldorn taking Weber's place as a character. (The Temple did appear in the *Black Mask* version but not until much later.) He also extensively reworked the ending of the story, improving it considerably.

Another element of interest relates to the final killer's identity; he turns out to be a long-time friend of the Op, novelist Owen Fitzstephan, who reveals himself as a Dain: "My mother and Gabrielle's maternal grandfather were brother and sister." He tells the Op that he will plead insanity, that "the cursed Dain blood" was in him, then adds, "It's no fun if I'm really cracked." He's judged insane and put away.

This is Hammett having his joke: the novelist naming a novelist as a mad villain, a self-indulgence for which he can be excused within such melodramatic surroundings. His portrait of Fitzstephan might well have served as self-description: " . . . a long, lean, sorrel-haired man of thirty-two with sleepy gray eyes, a wide, humorous mouth, and carelessly worn clothes; a man who pretended to be lazier than he was, would rather talk than do anything else and had a lot of what seemed to be accurate information and original ideas on any subject that happened to come up, as long as it was a little out of the ordinary."

In a letter of that period Hammett had described himself as "long and lean and gray-headed and very lazy [with] no ambition, no recreations." It was well known that he loved good talk, since Shaw reported that "long and fasci-

nating were the discussions between Whit [Raoul Whitfield] and Dash. . . ." And Mrs. Whitfield later recalled that her husband and Hammett "talked shop endlessly . . . debating whether a story should have seven murders or twenty-seven." (As for recreations, Hammett was a compulsive gambler—cards and crap games—loved prize fights, and hunted when he could afford to "up in northern Idaho and northwestern Montana . . . made to order for deer, elk and bear in season.")

By the time *The Dain Curse* had ended its run in *Black Mask*, Shaw was gloating over the fact that circulation had increased—during a single year—by 30,000. And, by August of 1929, another excellent Op novelet, "Fly Paper," was printed in the magazine.

With his financial condition improved (he had also been reviewing mystery novels for *The Saturday Review*), Hammett moved into a better neighborhood on Nob Hill, to a gable-windowed apartment house at 1155 Leavenworth, a few blocks west of the Mark Hopkins, with a panoramic view of downtown San Francisco. It was here he would write his most famous story, *The Maltese Falcon*, and by September the first installment of this revolutionary five-part serial would appear in the pages of *Black Mask*.

6

HAMMETT'S BLACK BIRD

Recalling the san francisco of Hammett, and *The Maltese Falcon,* veteran columnist Herb Caen vividly described the gritty atmosphere of this fog-haunted northern California city: "The Hall of Justice was dirty and reeked of evil. The criminal lawyers were young and hungry and used every shyster trick. . . . The City Hall, the D.A. and the cops ran the town as though they owned it, and they did. Hookers worked upstairs, not on the street; there were hundreds, maybe thousands, most of them named Sally. The two biggest abortion mills—one on Market the other on Fillmore—were so well-known they might as well have had neon signs. You could play roulette in the Marina, roll craps on O'Farrell, play poker on Mason, get rolled at 4 A.M. in a bar on Eddy, and wake up at noon in a Turk Street hotel with a girl whose name you never knew or cared to know. . . . San Francisco was a Sam Spade city."

And Sam Spade, the satan-faced private eye, was Dashiell Hammett's man—the cool, untrickable lone sleuth who stood between the law and lawbreakers, despised by both, respected by both, who could deal from the top or bottom of the deck, as occasion demanded, who grinned at loaded guns and told politicians and cops to go to hell, who bluffed, cracked wise, bedded his women, and handled his booze, who called San Francisco "my burg," and knew

every hood in it, a man of cynical humor, direct action and a man, above all else, who followed the ritual code of his profession.

"When a man's partner is killed he's supposed to do something about it," he says, after his agency co-partner, Miles Archer, is gunned down in the fog. What he does about it, and to whom, forms the backbone of Hammett's most famous novel, the prototype of a thousand others, the book which in the very act of remaking its field transcends it. Many critics have called it the finest crime novel ever written; certainly it is one of the half-dozen best, a classic which *The New Republic* (in a 1930 review) cited for its "absolute distinction of real art."

Editor Joseph Shaw, reading the 65,000-word manuscript in 1929 as a five-part serial, enthused to his readers: "In all of my experience I have never encountered a story as intense, as gripping or as powerful as this one. . . . It is a magnificent piece of writing. With all the earnestness of which I am capable, I tell you not to miss it."

The Maltese Falcon is remarkable in many respects. Aside from a bit of scuffling and a punch or two, all of the violence takes place offstage; the four killings are done "out of range," and we are shown the effects of murder rather than its execution, what its factual existence does to the men and women who share in it. Hammett gives us implied violence; guns are drawn and flourished, never fired; threats are made, tempers flare, accusations and cross-accusations abound—but Hammett keeps the tension taut as a stretched wire without ever resorting to overt violence. This is all the more fascinating in a book which most readers recall as "full of action and death." (Jacobi, the doomed ship's captain staggers into Sam's office and dies there, but he has been shot elsewhere; his ship has burned beyond our vision; we are shown only the end result of what has been done to him.) There is the constant, immediate feeling that, at any given moment, the scene will literally ex-

plode into bullets and blood, but Hammett resists the temptation, and suspense is therefore greatly intensified. Even at the climax, when one expects the usual shootout we are given only conversation—crackling, menace-laden conversation, laced with double and triple meaning—designed to do the job we have come to expect from overt violence. When the fat man, Gutman, is finally killed by one of his own gang we learn this as it is reported to Spade—just as we learned of the deaths of Archer and Thursby. And Spade, a man of violence, uses only his personality, his shrewdness, to hold the game in check. (Admittedly, in the course of the book, he disarms two of Gutman's hoods, but casually and with no fuss. Unlike the Op, he does not carry a gun, use a gun. Yet, always there is the feeling that he *would* use it—if he had to—as casually as he swats the pistol out of Cairo's grasp.)

The Maltese Falcon, when closely studied, is basically a series of brilliant dialogues, set in motion and bolstered by offstage events. The book could easily be translated into stage drama, with no more than minor cutting needed for the new form. The sets are all there: Spade's office, the girl's apartment, the fat man's hotel room where the last-act climax is played.

The characters in *Falcon* are etched so deeply that once encountered they cannot be forgotten: Casper Gutman, the florid fat man seeking the elusive gold-and-jewel-encrusted statuette, who speaks effusively in a "throaty purr" and whose eyes are "dark gleams in ambush behind pink puffs of flesh," who finds the resourceful Spade a more-than-worthy opponent; red-haired, blue-eyed Brigid O'Shaughnessy, the culmination of Hammett's good-evil women, the lying temptress who changes identity as often as she changes her old lies for new ones; Joel Cairo, the soft-voiced, perfumed homosexual; Wilmer Cook, the sadistic, baby-faced gunman; and Sam Spade himself, with his V-shaped face

and sharp predator's teeth ("He looked . . . like a blond satan and grinned . . . showing his jaw teeth").

Effective, too, is Effie Perine, Sam's secretary—and Lieutenant Dundy and detective Polhaus of Homicide, the coppers who dog Spade closely throughout the narrative. ("I've warned you your foot was going to slip one of these days," Dundy tells the detective. Spade remains unruffled. "It's a long while since I burst out crying because policemen didn't like me.")

The author had real people in mind when he created these characters (as he so often did with his detective fiction): "I followed Gutman's original in Washington," stated Hammett, "and I never remember shadowing a man who bored me so much. He was not after a jeweled falcon, of course; but he *was* suspected of being a German spy. Brigid was based, in part, on a woman who came in to Pinkerton's to hire an operative to discharge her housekeeper. [And, although Hammett didn't say so, she was also patterned on the advertising artist he'd shared an office with in San Francisco, Peggy O'Toole.] I worked with Dundy's prototype in a North Carolina railroad yard. The Cairo character I picked up on a forgery charge in 1920. Effie, the good girl, once asked me to go into the narcotic smuggling business with her in San Diego. Wilmer, the gunman was picked up in Stockton, California, a neat small smooth-faced quiet boy of perhaps twenty-one. He was serenely proud of the name the papers gave him—The Midget Bandit. He'd robbed a Stockton filling station the previous week—and had been annoyed by the description the station proprietor had given of him and by the proprietor's statement of what he would do to that little runt if he ever laid eyes on him again. So he'd stolen a car and returned to stick the guy up again and see what he wanted to do about it. That's when we nabbed him."

Hammett's detective, in this novel, bears his own first

name, Samuel, but the author denied autobiographical intent, declaring that "Spade had no original," that he was "idealized . . . in the sense that he is what most of the private detectives I've worked with would *like* to have been." The average detective, stated Hammett, cares nothing for the Sherlock Holmes image: "He wants to be a hard and shifty fellow, able to take care of himself in any situation, able to get the best of anybody he comes in contact with."

Hammett used several disguised San Francisco hotels in the course of the novel. Casper Gutman lives at the St. Mark, "a combination of the St. Francis and the Mark Hopkins." Cairo lives at the Belvedere, which was "based on the Bellevue."

Hammett's cross-and-double-cross scene writing reached its apex with the hotel room sequence wherein Sam tells Gutman that they must rig a "fall guy" for the police to pin all the murders on. He suggests the boy, Wilmer, and although Gutman is shocked ("I feel towards Wilmer just exactly as if he were my own son") the fat man considers the idea. Meanwhile, Spade offers to make Cairo the fall guy, and when the little man protests and says, "Suppose we give them . . . Miss O'Shaughnessy," Spade agrees that if "she could be rigged" he's willing to discuss that idea. She is horrified—and the boy is finally chosen. This entire sequence, in which Spade plays off one member of the gang against another, weakening all of them, sowing mistrust and hatred, is Hammett at his most masterful; his control is superb, and the scene could not be improved upon.

At Tony's Bar in New York, a few years after the book was published, Hammett told James Thurber that *Falcon* had been influenced by Henry James' *The Wings of the Dove*. "In both novels," related Thurber, "a fabulous fortune—jewels in *Falcon*, inherited millions in *Dove*—shapes the destinies of the disenchanted central characters, and James' designing woman, Kate Croy, like Hammett's

pistol-packing Brigid O'Shaughnessy, loses her lover in a Renunciation Scene."

The late W. Somerset Maugham, who basically admired Hammett's work, found Spade to be ". . . a nasty bit of goods . . . an unscrupulous rogue and a heartless crook. . . . There is little to choose between him and the criminals he is dealing with."

Yet this is precisely the character Spade wants to project to Gutman; it is imperative that the fat man think him capable of anything; he must play villain to defeat a villain. Later he says, to Brigid, "Don't be too sure I'm as crooked as I'm supposed to be. That kind of reputation [makes it] easier to deal with the enemy."

Actually, Spade wears many masks throughout the book—pretending to go along with the girl although he knows she killed Archer; stringing the police; working himself into a false rage for Gutman's benefit—and as each mask is removed a new one appears; total honesty is a luxury Sam cannot afford. The masks must remain in place. ("Everybody has something to conceal," he says.)

It would be a mistake to judge Spade as "unscrupulous" and "heartless." In the climactic sequence in which he finally turns Brigid over to the police he reveals the emotions of a man whose heart is with the woman, but whose code forbids his accepting her. Spade knows that he cannot continue to function if he breaks his personal code and goes off with Brigid—even while he admits that Miles Archer was "a louse" and that the agency is better off without him. Sam can sleep with Iva, the dead man's wife; he can bed down his secretary (". . . his hand on her hip. . . . 'Don't touch me now—not now.' ") and he can spend the night with Brigid, but he must never make a permanent alliance with any of them, the good or the evil. He must remain, like the Op, a free lance for hire. He may love Brigid ("I think I do") but he cannot trust love any more than he can trust the girl herself ("I am a liar," she tells him, "I

have always been a liar"). Spade refuses to "play the sap" for her, giving her all the code reasons for turning her in, then admits that after she's jailed "I'll have some rotten nights." Finally, emotionally, he tells her he won't let her go free "because all of me wants to—wants to say to hell with the consequences and do it—and because—God damn you—you've counted on that with me the same as you counted on that with the others."

This is not Maugham's heartless crook; this is a shaken man fully aware that emotion can destroy him if he lets it. Spade ultimately rejects Brigid, "sends her over," with the outwardly cruel and cynical line (which may have helped deceive Mr. Maugham): "You're an angel . . . [and] if they hang you I'll always remember you." Spade meant it literally.

But if not a villain neither was Sam Spade a hero. In fact, Hammett was presenting a new breed of anti-hero, a man whose rigid personal code is placed above that of the society he inhabits. He becomes, in effect, the individual lawmaker, a danger to any society. And Spade *is* a dangerous man, capable of using the corruption around him, admitting that "most things in San Francisco can be bought or taken."

In the midst of the case Spade tells Brigid a long, seemingly irrelevant story she does not understand, about a man named Flitcraft who left his wife and family suddenly one day, starting a whole new life—all because, while walking along the street, he had narrowly missed being killed by a falling beam, and "he felt like somebody had taken the lid off life and let him look at the works." Spade is telling the girl, in parable, that life is a series of falling beams and that some of us find out about them and some don't. He is telling Brigid, in effect, not to be surprised when one hits her—as it finally does. Spade lives longer because he knows the beams are falling, and is watching for them.

Ceremony helps hold Sam's world together. He follows

a stylized pattern in handling small details (the rolling of a cigarette, the ritual handshake, etc.) so that he may deal creatively with larger ones. Order within disorder. Mysticism mixed with hard practicality. Yet no more mysterious than Hemingway's war veteran (and Spade is a veteran of many wars) ceremoniously fishing on the Big Two-Hearted River. It is pertinent to note that in his magazine-to-book revisions Hammett substituted "They shook hands ceremoniously" for "They shook hands with marked formality." This same calming ceremony is present in the way Spade dresses, ransacks an apartment, disarms a gunman.

Novelist Kenneth Millar sees in the search for the jeweled falcon "a fable of modern man. . . . The black bird is hollow, worthless. The reality behind appearances is a treacherous vacuum. . . . The bird's lack of value implies Hammett's final comment on the inadequacy and superficiality of Spade's life and ours. If only his bitterly inarticulate struggle for self-realization were itself more fully realized . . . Sam Spade could have been a great indigenous tragic figure. . . . I think *The Maltese Falcon,* with its astonishing imaginative energy persisting undiminished after more than a third of a century, is tragedy of a new kind, deadpan tragedy."

Critic Allen Eyles termed it "a study of a group of people affected by the weakness of greed, realized with a force and a psychological aptness that gives it a moral purpose."

Hammett's involved blood history of the falcon, as told to Spade by Gutman, was partially—as with the characters themselves—based on fact. The author stated that "somewhere I had read of the peculiar rental agreement between Charles V and the Order of the Hospital of St. John of Jerusalem." He refers to the agreement of 1530 between the Order and Emperor Charles V, under which, as "rent" for the island of Malta (then under Spanish rule), they would pay Charles an annual tribute of a single falcon.

One of the birds they gave, according to Hammett's account, was "a glorious golden falcon encrusted from head to foot with the finest jewels in their coffers." It moves from country to country down the years, leaving a trail of death and theft and deceit, until Gutman goes after it some seventeen years before the story opens. It is against this highly romantic background that Hammett plays out what editor Shaw called his "saga of a private detective."

That the bird is a worthless fake when Gutman finally gets it is no real surprise to Spade. He never believed in it anyhow; men who live in seedy apartments and work out of seedy office buildings may dream of fabled riches, but they know such riches will not be seen in their lifetime. Gutman is crushed (by the falling beam), but Spade is safe and free to continue as before, lonely, embittered, but able to function on a realistic level. He still has his job. He's been "through it all before" and expects to go through it again.

In 1929, when Hammett wrote *Falcon*, rather strong editorial censorship existed in the popular magazines. When Hammett's serial arrived Shaw checked it carefully. Sex came first. Brigid's line, "I'm not ashamed to be naked before you," was dropped, as was a line from Cairo directed to her regarding a boy she had failed to sleep with. ("The one you couldn't make.") A damn or a hell was permitted, but outright swearing or foul language was not. (Hammett got around this neatly, losing none of the intended impact. "The boy spoke two words, the first a short guttural verb, the second 'you.' ") Hammett's line from Spade, "How long have you been off the gooseberry lay, son?" was changed to "How long have you been off the lay?" since Shaw was certain Hammett had something dark in mind. Actually, "the gooseberry lay" was crook slang for stealing wash from a clothesline!

However, Shaw did not touch the line "Keep that gunsel away from me . . ." because he assumed the word

"gunsel" meant gunman. He was wrong. It was a homosexual term, meaning "a kept boy." Yet, to this day, mystery writers continue to misuse it, following Shaw's line of thought as to its origin.

Homosexuality in general was not censored nearly as much as heterosexuality in those early pulp days. In the book version, when Spade questions a house detective about Joel Cairo, the man answers with a leer, "Oh, that one." The original magazine version was bolder in the detective's reply, "Oh, *her*!"

Another interesting Hammett magazine-to-book change, having nothing to do with censorship but dealing with clarity, consisted of his switching "You'll want to sleep if you've been in the grease all night" to "You'll want to sleep if you've been standing up under a police storm all night." Hammett was always working to improve his writing for hard-cover publication.

The Maltese Falcon became an immediate best seller (surpassed only by *The Thin Man* in overall sales through the years). In *Falcon's* first decade and a half the book saw two dozen hard-cover printings in three separate editions. Fifteen of these printings were issued out of Modern Library.

With the successful publication of *Red Harvest, The Dain Curse,* and now with *The Maltese Falcon,* Samuel Dashiell Hammett had achieved a major critical and financial breakthrough.

7

A SHATTERED KEY AND AN EARLY THIN MAN

THE DEPRESSION YEARS were beginning in America. The "lawless decade" was taking its toll. Prohibition and gangland wars had ravaged the cities, and the stock market crash in October of 1929 was the killing blow for a weakened nation. By 1930 there were block-long bread lines in the streets of New York.

For Hammett, the situation was fortunately reversed. Warner's was interested in buying *The Maltese Falcon*; his publisher, Alfred Knopf, had paid a solid advance against Hammett's next novel, and royalty checks were coming in regularly on his first three books. Alfred's wife, Blanche, was responsible for bringing hard-boiled writing to Knopf. She appreciated good crime fiction, and fostered Hammett, Raymond Chandler, and James M. Cain—as well as Benjamin Appel and Raoul Whitfield. Her pioneering influence lent needed respectability to the hard-boiled novel.

After the breakup of his marriage, Hammett had moved from San Francisco to New York, and was now on the staff of the *Evening Post*, as mystery reviewer. Covering crime novels from early April through October of that year, Hammett was rough on most of his contemporaries.

Of Octavus Roy Cohen: "a clumsily managed mystery, full of . . . bad writing."

Of Rupert Hughes: "It is written in Mr. Hughes' unfortunate later style, hysterically, at the top of his voice."

Of Mary Roberts Rinehart: "cluttered . . . confusing . . . it is simply impossible to believe in the arch-criminal."

Of Edgar Wallace: ". . . at his most naively melodramatic."

And of his old "enemy" S. S. Van Dine: ". . . as incomparably inefficient, as amazingly ignorant as ever." (Hammett was here referring to Van Dine's two police inspectors.)

Yet, he liked Philip MacDonald's *The Noose*, stating, "It is logical, it is simple, it is baffling." And he had high praise for Raoul Whitfield's *Green Ice* (another *Black Mask* story published by Knopf): "The plot does not matter. . . . What matters is that here are 280 pages of naked action pounded into tough compactness by staccato, hammerlike writing." Hammett was being too kind; Whitfield's book, unlike *Falcon*, has dated badly and could not be profitably reprinted today. The style was too tough, too staccato, lacking the control that Hammett brought to his fiction. Whitfield was of the period; Hammett transcended it.

Whit and Dash continued to talk shop in New York. A mutual friend reported one of their conversations: "Whitfield maintained that—given characters and a general plot—it was a cinch to write a detective story; when in a spot, all one need do is use well-known props. A good writer should produce a novel without any of these appurtenances to achieve effect. And Hammett's comeback: 'All right, Whit, if you want to make it the hard way, try writing a book omitting every word that has the letter 'f' for example.' "

Erle Stanley Gardner (writing in *The Atlantic*) recalls Hammett in this period. Needing immediate cash, Hammett took a story to a Manhattan magazine editor, put it on his desk and asked him to read it.

"Now?" asked the astonished editor.

"Now," said Hammett. "If you don't like it, I'll take it somewhere else."

As Hammett eyed him warily, the editor read the story. He nodded. "We'll buy it."

"Fine," said Hammett. "I'll take the check."

"Now?" asked the editor.

"You pay on acceptance, don't you?"

"Well . . . yes, but our checks don't go out until—"

"I'll take mine now."

The check was issued. As Hammett put it into his wallet the editor casually pointed out a few alterations needed in the manuscript. "We'll handle them," he said.

"Oh, no." Hammett snatched up his story. "*I'll* handle them."

He stalked from the office—with check *and* manuscript.

According to Gardner, as soon as Hammett cashed the check he stocked up on his favorite alcoholic beverage and disappeared.

Weeks passed.

The nervous editor, who had featured Hammett's name on the cover of the new issue, could not locate the author. He had a cover, but no story. Just before the final press deadline the editor frantically ordered his office staff to begin pasting printed slips over Hammett's name. Several hundred of these magazine covers had been doctored when a taxi driver arrived with a large envelope for the editor. The Hammett manuscript was inside, neatly corrected. Now all the editor had to do was send it to the printer and steam off several hundred cover slips.

"Dash was a hell-for-leather drinker in those days," says a friend, recalling this particular incident. "But he always kept his word. Had a real *thing* about keeping his word. He sobered up just long enough to edit that story in a speakeasy, then paid a cab driver to deliver it. The wor-

ried editor needn't have worried. Dash always met his deadlines."

Another major Hammett novel was soon in print: beginning in March of 1930, as a series of four segments, *The Glass Key* appeared in *Black Mask*. The background was, once again, political corruption, with part of the action set in New York. Hammett later named *Key* his personal favorite among his books. In trying to break away from the confining characterization of a detective hero he created Ned Beaumont, a man very much like Hammett himself, even to appearance. Beaumont, like his creator, was tall and lean and wore a mustache; he was a compulsive, destructive gambler (dice, cards, horses); he drank; he suffered from tuberculosis; he was hard, cynical, and loyal. Beaumont worked for a political boss, Paul Madvig, and had been with him a year when the story begins. He is told by Mrs. Madvig, Paul's mother, "You're the best friend he's ever had." But is he? Hammett never delves into their true relationship; he keeps the reader at a distance. Critical speculation on the closeness of the Beaumont-Madvig duo has run the gamut from homosexuality to a father-son relationship—but it is relatively safe to assume that Hammett meant to convey a deep man-to-man friendship.

The Glass Key is a perplexing, frustrating book. Here, Hammett himself wears the Spade mask; we are never allowed inside any of the people he writes about; we see them all once-removed; we are forced to judge them strictly on what they say and do. Hammett never used the objective approach more stringently.

We see Beaumont picked up by Madvig's political enemies; he is offered money by Shad O'Rory to betray Madvig. Beaumont seems to go along with the idea, accepting the money. But he wants to leave; O'Rory wants him to stay. On this physical basis, not on any apparent moral one, Beaumont throws the money at O'Rory. Ham-

mett then delivers one of the most brutal sequences ever written, wherein Beaumont is beaten back from the door again and again by O'Rory's apelike henchman, Jeff. Shad wants the information on Madvig, but Beaumont refuses to speak. He is beaten savagely until, to quote Jeff, "It ain't no good now. He's throwed another joe." (Meaning he is no longer conscious.) They bring him to, keep beating him. In his blood-weary state Beaumont tries to kill himself, but is finally found by police and taken to a hospital. Did he suffer this agony out of loyalty to his friend, or because his ego was threatened? Would he have walked out with O'Rory's money and laughed about it with Madvig, or would he have sent O'Rory the damaging information he wanted? Or is Beaumont really "a damned massacrist" as Jeff calls him? We don't know. Hammett does not tell us. There is much he does not tell us.

The "love scene" at the book's end is equally ambiguous. Senator Ralph Henry's daughter, Janet, who has been linked with Madvig through the course of the book, suddenly decides to run off with Beaumont in the last two pages. Her father has been revealed as a murderer by Beaumont (functioning as amateur sleuth) and she does not love Paul Madvig. Yet, she does not say she loves Beaumont, nor does he express any kind of affection for her. Their cool exchange (in condensed form):

> "You don't like me. . . ."
>
> "You're all right," he said, "only you're not right for Paul . . . I tried to tell him that."
>
> "You despise me," she said.
>
> "I don't despise you," he said irritably. . . . "I'll have to say goodbye now."
>
> She held her hands out impulsively. "Take me with you."
>
> "Do you really want to go or are you just

> being hysterical? . . . I'll take you if you want to go. . . ."

When Paul comes to Ned's apartment to say goodbye the girl is there. Ned tells him, "Janet is going away with me." Madvig is struck hard by this news; he staggers from the room, and Hammett ends his novel with the girl looking at Beaumont while "he stared fixedly at the door."

Is it Hammett's intention to imply that Beaumont does not really care for Janet, that he is taking her because he feels she's "not right for Paul," or is it that the two have fallen in love offstage (à la the violence in *Falcon*) and that Hammett is here showing us the end result of their feelings? The book is full of such ambiguous scenes, and we are never certain just where Beaumont stands in relation to Paul Madvig or Janet Henry.

Ned Beaumont is another of Hammett's code characters, but his is not the code of Spade or the Op. He says, "I can stand anything I've got to stand," and proves this with Jeff and O'Rory. When the girl asks him if he believes in dreams, he tells her no. "I don't believe in anything, but I'm too much of a gambler not to be affected by a lot of things." (Compare this to a letter Hammett once wrote in which he declares, "If you have fooled around with crap games as much as I have, you know what chance can do to the laws of probabilities.") Again, when she tells him, "I know you're a gentleman . . ." he corrects her, "You're wrong. I'm a gambler and a politician's hanger-on."

Early in the novel, when his bookie (a man named Despain) "blows town" with Beaumont's track winnings, Ned begs Madvig to put him on as a special deputy so he can go after the bookie with a gun.

"What good am I if my luck's gone? [With this win] I can take my tail out from between my legs and feel that I'm a person again and not just something that's being

kicked around. The money's important enough, but it's not the real thing. It's what losing and losing and losing does to me. . . . If I stand for it, I'm licked, my nerve's gone. . . . I'm going after him. I've got to."

Beaumont's code demands this action, and he gets the badge and gun, and nails Despain in New York. Thus, he can continue to function (as Spade continues, after turning in Brigid); the code has been observed. You don't let life step on you if you can help it; if you can't (bad luck) then you learn to take it.

Hammett's title comes from a dream told by Janet Henry. Janet and Ned are together, and very hungry. They reach a house with food inside, but it is locked. There is a glass key with which to open the door, but in doing so they would release a roomful of snakes writhing on the floor. In her first recounting of the dream Janet lies to Ned, telling him that they escaped the snakes and ate the food—but he does not believe her happy ending. Then, when they are going away together at the end, she reveals the truth: that the glass key shattered and that "we couldn't lock the snakes in, and they came out all over us."

Hammett is telling us that they are in for a bad time, that they should not have fed their "hunger," for soon the snakes will overtake them. (If Spade had fed his hunger for Brigid, the snakes would surely have had him.)

The book is full of good sharp descriptive writing: "Long oyster-colored lines of rain slanted down into China Street. . . . At her left was a hawk-nosed long-chinned pale man, a predatory animal of forty. . . . Jeff was jovially cursing the two detectives who held him. Every time he cursed, one of the detectives struck him in the face with his fist. Jeff laughed and kept on cursing them. His false teeth had been knocked out. His mouth bled."

The core of the book is the Madvig-Beaumont friendship, which is never stable. Just prior to the O'Rory beating, Beaumont is with Paul in a bar, when they come to blows

over a difference of opinion; Beaumont seems ready to kill Madvig, but pulls back at the last second. Yet, later in the story, when Paul has confessed to a murder (a false confession, but one which is accepted at that moment) Beaumont stands fast by him. "You're right about my being Paul's friend," he tells Janet. "I'm that no matter who he killed."

We must guess what Ned Beaumont is feeling ("his eyes gave no indication of what he thought"). Hammett plays his fictional cards close to the chest; we never learn as much as we'd like to learn.

In a long essay discussing Hammett and his work, David T. Bazelon states: "*The Glass Key* . . . is Hammett's chief attempt at a genuine novel. . . . Ned Beaumont is [the author's] closest, most serious projection . . . yet we never know whether Beaumont's motive in solving the murder is loyalty, job-doing, or love . . . this ambiguity reflects, I think, Hammett's difficulty in writing an unformularized novel—one in which an analysis of motives is fundamental."

Robert Edenbaum, for basically the same reasons, called *The Glass Key* Hammett's "least satisfactory novel . . . [in Hemingway] the mask is lifted every time the character is alone; he admits his misery to himself . . . exposes his inner life. The Hammett mask is never lifted; the Hammett character never lets you inside. Instead of the potential despair of Hemingway, Hammett gives you unimpaired control and machinelike efficiency."

Yet Louis Untermeyer declared, "Hammett has done something extraordinarily new to the murder and mystery story. He has made the reader as much interested in the relation of his individuals to each other as in the solution of the story."

Somerset Maugham saw, in Ned Beaumont, "a curious, intriguing character whom any novelist would have been proud to conceive."

And Raymond Chandler found "an effect of movement, intrigue, cross-purposes, and the gradual elucidation of character, which is all the detective story has any right to be about anyway. All the rest is spillikins in the parlor."

As with his other *Black Mask* novels, Hammett worked *Key* over carefully for book format. In one of the magazine segments he'd referred to a racehorse as "Ruthless Raoul," but changed it in the book to "Pipe-organ." Hammett was, of course, having some fun with Whitfield's name in the magazine. He would occasionally do this: in an unpublished manuscript he referred to "police magistrate Erle Gardner"—and in a short story to "a boxer named Kid Perelman." Both S. J. Perelman and Erle Stanley Gardner were old friends. It is not uncommon for authors to engage in such leg-pulling. In fact, Perelman's "Farewell, My Lovely Appetizer" is a very funny parody of both Hammett and Chandler.

The *Black Mask* era was ending for Dashiell Hammett. Only one other Hammett story appeared in the magazine, "Death and Company," the last of the Continental Op series. (Although Joe Shaw wrote many letters urging Hammett to revive the Op—and once enclosed a $500 check as an advance against a story—this case marked the fat detective's final bow.)

In seven years Hammett had produced three dozen Op titles, all of which were eventually gathered into book form, with ten of the series forming his three Op novels, and the other twenty-six short stories and novelets being spread over eight paperbacks. (All but two of the Op series had appeared originally in *Black Mask*.)

That farewell Hammett issue was dated November, 1930, almost eight years to the month since Hammett had first appeared in *Black Mask*. He'd been in more than fifty issues, and no other writer had made such an impact on the magazine. Shaw was bragging to the end: "We knew he was great . . . but it took the *Black Mask* stories published

in book form to wake up the country as to how great he really is."

When he left the magazine, Hammett was at the top of the readers' listings, leading Daly, Gardner, Nebel, and Whitfield.

During 1930, working out of New York (at 133 East 38th Street), he began a new San Francisco detective story.

Written in the objective third person style of *Key*, this unfinished novel (of some 18,000 words) centers around the case of a missing scientist-philosopher who has "apparently" shot his secretary to death and vanished. Hammett's detective in the case, John Guild of Associated Detective Bureaus, Inc. in San Francisco, does not believe that the scientist is guilty, and sets out to prove it. With Guild, Hammett created a sleuth who combined the businesslike Agency approach of the Op and the ultra coolness of Spade. As with Ned Beaumont, we are given no hint of his inner feelings, his thoughts on the case. Hammett continually refers to him as "the dark man," and one character—a night-club drunk—accuses him of being "a damn mulatto." Guild drinks beer, carries a gun, chainsmokes, has blue eyes and a sun-darkened complexion. That's all Hammett reveals about him; these facts and his Op-like working philosophy. When Elsa Fremont attempts to seduce him and he does not respond she calls him "bloodless," a "ghost" of a man, declaring that he is "unreal, untouchable . . . trying to really come in contact with you is just like trying to hold a handful of smoke." He is coldly amused. "It's an advantage when I'm working," he says.

The only sequence which saw commercial use in this unpublished manuscript was a brief section set in Chinatown wherein the detective meets the brother of a man he sent to prison. Hammett used this scene, in revised form, for his film original, "After the Thin Man," written later in Hollywood. Also, he used the last names of two of the characters, Guild and Wynant, and the first name of the

Sheriff, Nick, as well as the sixty-five-page fragment's title, "The Thin Man," when he wrote the classic Nick Charles novel three years later.

"I knew [it] could not be published until the fall of 1931," Hammett stated, in writing about this manuscript. "So—having plenty of time—I put these sixty-five pages aside and went to Hollywood. One thing and/or another intervening . . . I didn't return to work on the story until a couple of more years had passed—and then I found it . . . generally more satisfactory to keep only the basic idea [of a disappearing scientist, described as a very thin man] and otherwise to start anew."

It is impossible to determine just how successful this unfinished novel would have been, but it bears very little resemblance, in plot or mood, to the published book of the same title. The light humor, zany man-wife relationship, weird characters, drinking, and sex all came later. This original version is stark and humorless; one can hardly imagine Asta barking his way into its dark pages.

Wisecracking, hard-drinking Nick Charles replaced grim, job-oriented John Guild.

8

HOLLYWOOD AND NICK CHARLES

HOLLYWOOD OF THE THIRTIES: California's Mad Hatter Eldorado, producing dreams wholesale for one hundred million people who sought weekly escape in the enchanted dark of a film palace; having spawned Mack Sennett and custard pies, Chaplin and the Keystone Cops, it was now moving rapidly into its Golden Age of Sound. It was Jean Harlow's town, the Hollywood of Hecht and MacArthur, the Barrymores, of Scott Fitzgerald and Gene Fowler, of panderers and pimps, of golden girls and gilt-edge grifters, where young Thalberg reigned at MGM and Benchley lived in the Garden of Allah; the town of Goldwyn and Gish and Garbo, the Marx Brothers and Dorothy Parker, of Selznick and Mayer and the Warner boys, of marbled mansions, bathtub gin, hookers and hard guys; the town of the cross and double-cross, of perjury and pleasure. It was everything the papers said it was, and more.

Ben Hecht had been there since 1925; he'd written the first popular gangster film, "Underworld" (which he'd followed with "Scarface"), and was noted for his ability to portray the world of crime on screen. In 1929 Paramount had taken an option on a new crime novel, *Red Harvest*, and they wanted Ben to put it into screen form. Hecht said okay, and did a treatment, changing the plot considerably. Then Garrett Fort took over, making more changes. The

film was released in 1930, with no official credit to Hammett's book, as "Roadhouse Nights," and featured the screen debut of a new comedian, Jimmy Durante. A trade paper called it "a nifty talker with . . . laughs and thrills."

That same year *The Maltese Falcon* was published by Knopf, and Warner Brothers bought it. Price: $8,500 for all rights. Not big money by Hollywood standards, but in the bread-line Depression years it seemed a considerable amount to its author. When Hammett got a call from the west coast, late in 1930, offering him screen work, he quickly accepted. He settled in at 1551½ North Bronson Avenue in Hollywood, and soon made friends with Ben Hecht.

The two writers shared interests. Ben had grown up in Chicago, been part of the Capone era, and Hammett was intrigued by his true stories of guns and gangsters. Hecht, on the other hand, relished the Pinkerton anecdotes recounted by Hammett.

"Of the thousand writers huffing and puffing through movieland," Hecht later wrote, "there were scarcely fifty men and women of wit or talent." Hecht recalled the era vividly: "Most of the important people got drunk after one o'clock, sobered up around three-thirty and got drunk again at nine. Fist fights began around eleven. Seduction had no stated hours, and the skimpy offices shook with passion. The mingled sounds of plotting and sexual moans came through the transoms."

Of the town itself, he wrote: "I remember fine homes with handsome butlers . . . vivid people, long and noisy luncheons, nights of gaiety and gambling, hotel suites and rented palaces overrun with friends, partners, secretaries. . . . I remember yelling matches in the lairs of the caliphs, swimming parties, all-night card games—and a picnic of money-making. . . . The town was loud with wild hearts and the poetry of success."

Hammett did not come to Hollywood directly from New York; he first made a stopover in Baltimore, Maryland,

to see his family. ("My father was still alive then.") They welcomed him as a "famous writer," and all the desperate job-to-job childhood years were forgotten. Hammett's surface display of happiness, however, covered a basic unrest, which would be heightened by his life in California. ("I drank a lot in those days—partly because I was confused by the fact that people's feelings and talk and actions didn't have much to do with one another.")

He was drinking in Hollywood when he met the woman he was to know and love for the next three decades of his life, playwright Lillian Hellman. She recalls their first meeting in a Hollywood restaurant; Hammett was just getting over a five-day drunk. She was immediately drawn to the tall thin man with "the wonderful face," and they talked of T.S. Eliot, the film industry, and a hundred other topics, sitting in Hammett's car until daylight.

Lillian Hellman was then the wife of Arthur Kober, whom she had married in 1925. Born in New Orleans in 1905, she was in her mid-twenties when she met Hammett, and had already written book reviews for the *Herald Tribune*, had been a manuscript and play reader in New York City, and had come to Hollywood that year (1930) to work in the story department at MGM as a scenario reader. She had decided to give up the struggle to write creatively and was attempting to adjust herself to judging the work of others. Hammett would have none of it; he told her that if she wanted to write she must not give up. If she turned out to be a bad writer, then she could quit; the world would not miss her. Listening to his "tough logic" and believing it, she began to write again. He attacked her work, page by page, showing her what was wrong, what was weak, what was false.

Hammett was also involved with other writers that season. In 1931, the same year in which *The Glass Key* was published in book form, he edited a horror anthology for The John Day Company, *Creeps By Night*, for which he

wrote the introduction and selected twenty tales of terror by William Faulkner, John Collier, Irvin S. Cobb, Conrad Aiken, Stephen Vincent Benét, André Maurois, Philip MacDonald, and others. Hammett's introductory remarks dealt with the reader's ability to believe in the supernormal, and he summed up by stating: "If you believe in werewolves, then it can make little difference to you, except perhaps academically, whether your heroine is eaten by one of them or shot down by a Cicero muscleman." Again, it was the practical Hammett onstage.

In Hollywood, he worked on several projects: a screen vehicle for Marlene Dietrich (which never reached production), a mystery for William Powell, "Divorce Detective," sponsored—but never produced—by Warner Brothers, and an original film treatment, "City Streets," produced by Paramount in 1931, starring Gary Cooper, and reviewed by the press as "probably the first sophisticated treatment of a gangster picture." That same year saw Warner Brothers bring out "The Maltese Falcon," adapted by a trio of screen writers from the Hammett novel, and starring Ricardo Cortez as Sam Spade, and Bebe Daniels as the lying girl.

"It was apparently planned as a vehicle for its male star," says Ron Goulart. "Cortez [whose real name was Jacob Kranz] was a sleepy-eyed lover with Valentino hair and Ramon Novarro postures. His Sam Spade was a strange hybrid, half-tough, half-sultry. In some scenes he is terse and cynical. In others he looks as if he's about to carry the heroine off into the desert. When Spade talks to the girl in his apartment he wears a silk lounging robe and sits before a giant roaring fireplace . . . hardly typical of Hammett's detective."

Hammett had nothing to do with this production, the first of three films to be made from his book. This initial version, directed by Roy del Ruth as a semi-comedy, was a box-office dud.

By the summer of 1932, as the nation entered the depth of the Depression (with fifteen million unemployed), Hammett was known in Hollywood as "one of the local characters." His sharp wit was often directed at friends. Of Dorothy Parker, he was quoted as saying: "Dorothy carries brass knuckles—on her tongue."

During this period, a major magazine piece on his life and work appeared in *The Bookman*. The entranced interviewer, Elizabeth Sanderson, described him as "tall, slim, sophisticated, with prematurely white hair above a young face. . . . Mr. Hammett wants to write a play. Later he will write straight novels, but not until he has written his play. . . . When he works his enthusiasm carries him through thirty-six hour periods of steady writing. . . . He plans to go abroad, wants to stay in Europe a year or two while he finishes his play."

Hammett never got to Europe, nor did he work on his play that summer. What he did do was attend parties, parties, parties. Ben Hecht, who hosted one of the wildest and gaudiest, later reminisced about it: "At that time we were living in a rented wooden castle on a Hollywood hill. Leland Hayward, our agent, Charles MacArthur, and I lived and worked there. There were two hundred and fifty turkeys on the grounds. There was a big mosaic fountain on the front terrace. The drawing room was large enough for a baseball diamond. We never counted the bedrooms. Two chefs in ballooning white hats cooked for us, and there was a printing press in the cellar on which we printed our dinner menus. We called the joint Turkey Hill . . . and we drank, swore, and sinned there."

It was to Turkey Hill that Hammett came that summer, striding up the grade with his long legs pumping, grinning happily at Ben and Charlie, who promptly led him to the bar. The Great Ones gathered: Jean Harlow, all sex and blazing blonde hair, holding the hand of her fiancé Paul Bern (who would, shortly thereafter, kill him-

self on their wedding night); John Gilbert, a soon-to-fade idol of the silent screen, with three whores he'd hired for the evening; Harpo Marx and Ernst Lubitsch playing craps; director Howard Hawks, listening with sad eyes as George Antheil stroked the piano; a young actress named Nora, who would later become Princess Von Starhemberg of Austria, being leered at by Myron Selznick. Bootleg booze and industry small talk flowed in equal measure. "The two drinkers out front were MacArthur and Hammett," recalled Hecht. "They took the lead early in the evening and were holding on to it without sign of strain. . . . Dash remembered a gun duel in San Francisco with a marijuana smoker. The party had climbed a high perch."

That same summer, in a Los Angeles courtroom, actress Elise de Viane won a damage suit against Hammett, after her lawyer proved, to the satisfaction of the court, that the defendant "made violent love to her." The fluttery-eyed Miss de Viane declared that she was shocked when, after accompanying Hammett to his apartment, he suggested more than drinks. She was awarded $2,500. (Just a few months later, Hammett was back in court, winning the decision in a suit against author C. Henderson, of London, whose novel, *Death in the Dark*, was said to be lifted directly from *The Maltese Falcon*.)

Hammett was extremely attractive to women during these Hollywood years, and he spent a fortune entertaining them. Money literally meant nothing to him. Hammett's marriage had long since disintegrated, although he still saw his two children. (Lillian Hellman obtained a divorce late in 1932 from Arthur Kober, but Hammett was not to be divorced until 1937).

Black Mask readers missed their favorite author. They constantly wrote editor Shaw, asking for new Hammett stories. In desperation, Shaw ran an editorial: "Dashiell Hammett's *Maltese Falcon* has been screened . . . his *Glass*

Key will also appear and be heard in movie-talkie theaters . . . we have many letters asking when he'll have another story for us. Our answer is 'maybe'—because when a fellow is pulling $100,000 a year out of Hollywood we just don't have the heart—or is it nerve?—to suggest that he knock off and turn us out one of those great old Continental Op stories. Anyway, we keep hoping."

Three new Hammett stories were printed in 1932, but for money Shaw could never afford to pay. Two appeared in *American Magazine* and one in *Collier's*. All three featured Hammett's already-famous Sam Spade, but lacked the bite and tension of *Falcon*. These "slick" magazines paid premium rates to get detective Spade into their pages, but the work was below par for Hammett, at best clean professional prose which did nothing to help or harm him as a writer. (One of the trio, "A Man Called Spade," was picked up for several anthologies and became one of his most-reprinted pieces, but this, too, lacked the depth and spark of the longer Spade work.) The stories were written to order, and in all three cases Spade seemed almost bored with his detecting.

Hammett completed his last published novel, *The Thin Man*, during 1933, and it became one of his greatest successes, resulting in several feature films, a popular radio show, and, eventually, a TV series. Nick and Nora Charles joined Tarzan, Dick Tracy, Buck Rogers, and a host of other characters who became part of the American way of life.

Hammett had not anticipated any such success when he sat down to write the novel; it was a matter of finishing the job he had started in 1930 (with the John Guild version) and of meeting a commitment to his publisher for a follow-up book to *The Glass Key*. The advance from Knopf was needed, since Hammett was once again strapped for money. (A fellow-writer of the period who knew Ham-

mett in Hollywood reported that "Dash was a compulsive gambler who wasted a great deal of the money that he earned from the studios.")

The Thin Man was written in the East, at a rundown New York hotel, The Sutton, managed by writer Nathanael West. Hammett worked in a three-room, rent-free section ironically dubbed "The Royal Suite," due to its cramped size. Lillian Hellman, who was there to witness the birth of *The Thin Man* (and to whom the book was dedicated) was amazed at Hammett's concentration and total dedication to the job at hand. "I had never seen anybody work that way: the care for every word, the pride in the neatness of the typed page itself, the refusal . . . to go out for a walk for fear something would be lost."

West's brother-in-law, S. J. Perelman, had purchased a home in Bucks County and invited them all down for a housewarming. Upon arrival, hanging up their coats and hats, they found a dead fish in the closet, which Perelman shrugged aside. ("This is fishing country.") It was here that Hammett shared hunting weekends with critic Robert Coates, West, and Perelman. They were sometimes joined by William Faulkner, who became a good friend to both Hellman and Hammett.

The Thin Man is narrated in the first person by ex-sleuth Nick Charles (Greek name: Charalambides), originally with the Trans-American Detective Agency of San Francisco, temporarily living in New York City. Hammett portrayed him as a charming, hard-drinking, funloving gentleman. That Nick was tough, in his heyday, is apparent, but the toughness has been replaced by cockiness; Nick refuses to take anything seriously unless backed to the wall. Nora, his equally funloving wife, does the backing. She gets him involved in the case against his will, forces him to use his intelligence to solve what another writer might have been tempted to call "The Case of the Vanishing Thin Man." (Later, of course, the public decided that Nick was

the "thin man," and he was thus tagged for all the movie sequels.)

Nick and Nora become involved with a cast of "man-eaters": Mimi Jorgensen, Nick's ex-flame, and a character written in the Hammett tradition of Brigid O'Shaughnessy ("When you catch her in a lie, she admits it and gives you another lie to take its place and, when you catch her in that one, admits it and gives you still another."); Dorothy Wynant ("cute, but cuckoo"), Mimi's daughter, who carries a rusted pistol in her purse; Gilbert, Mimi's neurotic, crime-obsessed son, who is interested in cannibalism; Herbert Macaulay, the crooked lawyer who has actually done away with the missing Wynant and who prefers to keep him "alive" for financial gain; Shep Morelli, a nervous gangster who almost kills Nick (". . . as I sprawled across the floor I caught one of his ankles and rolled over with it, bringing him down on me, and he clubbed my back with the gun . . ."); Studsy Burke, who runs the Pig-iron Club ("Studsy leaned over . . . and smashed a big fist into the fat man's face. . . . 'I ain't running a dive, but I ain't trying to run a young ladies' seminary neither!' "). Hammett used the original name of his detective, John Guild, for a police lieutenant called into the case, but this character bears no relationship to "the dark man" from Hammett's unfinished first-draft manuscript.

Nora is delighted with the entire caper. ("I love you, Nicky, because you smell nice and know such fascinating people.") But when Nick gets serious he discards such chatter and admits that he's worried by "riddles and lies—and I'm too old and too tired for them to be any fun." He wants to get back to San Francisco. But at the end, he's changed his mind again. The old habits have returned. "Let's stick around awhile," he says to Nora. "This excitement has put us behind in our drinking."

When *The Thin Man* was sent out for pre-book sale to the major magazines none of them would touch the

manuscript. "Too daring," they complained—until the editor of *Redbook*, Edwin Balmer, liked it and bought the story. However, he, too, was shocked by certain words—in particular, by a question which Nora asks Nick after he's tussled with an attractive woman. "Tell me the truth: when you were wrestling with Mimi, didn't you have an erection?" And he answers: "Oh, a little."

"Such a question had never before reached my desk as part of a literary production," Balmer primly declared. He got out his blue pencil and drew a line through the offending dialogue.

Redbook published the story, condensed somewhat, in its December, 1933, issue, and when the magazine money arrived Hammett moved to a remote fishing spot in the Florida Keys, staying through the spring and summer. His love of wild places, of lakes and woods and isolated cabins, was nurtured in the Keys; the furor of New York publishing was forgotten.

Shortly after the book appeared in its Knopf hardcover edition Sinclair Lewis stated that "Dashiell Hammett is undoubtedly the best of American detective story writers, and *The Thin Man* is certainly the most breathless of his stories." Alexander Woollcott called it "the best detective story yet written in America." Herschel Brickell, another noted literary authority, spoke of "the punch of Mr. Hammett's streamlined dialogue," adding that the novel was "ace writing, much too good to be missed, whether you like detective stories or not." The most sustained rave came from England, from the *New Statesman and Nation*, which noted that "Dashiell Hammett is almost alone in being praised by writers as a serious writer and by good novelists as a master of their business. Hemingway continues to admire him . . ." The reviewer went on to call the novel "absorbing and extremely ingenious [with] lurid glimpses of New York drinking society, but . . . what will the British public say of a detective—now happily married—who has

once had 'immoral relations' with the woman he suspects of having murdered her divorced husband's mistress and confidante?—whose first thought, when he wakes up in the middle of the night, is to ask his wife to pour him a whiskey and soda?"

The British public loved it, as did the American public. By January 30th, 1934, Knopf had taken out a curious ad in *The New York Times* in which the publisher stated: "We don't believe the question on page 192 ["... didn't you have an erection?"] of Dashiell Hammett's *The Thin Man* has had the slightest influence upon the sale of the book. It takes more than that to make a best seller these days. Twenty thousand people don't buy a book within three weeks to read a five-word question."

Editor Balmer was upset by the ad, and wrote a piece in which he spoke of the shocking "new candor" of modern publishers, exemplified by the printed Hammett phrase which he had blue-penciled out of *Redbook*. "My own magazine cannot be accused of being crinoline-minded," he wrote, "but we seem to be welcoming a common condition of literary nudism."

Howard Haycraft, writing in *Murder for Pleasure*, called Hammett's saga of Nick and Nora Charles "his least typical and least important contribution," but also made the point that the novel was "not without significance on its own account, as one of the first works to bring humor, of a distinctly native brand, to the detective story in this country."

Hammett had changed considerably since 1930, when he began the first version of *The Thin Man* (with *Black Mask* in mind). John Guild, his dark, morose, job-holding detective would have rejected the spoiled lumber heiress and her millions (Nick quits the detective business to marry Nora and manage her properties), and he would certainly never drink before breakfast. The job-holder was replaced by the partygoer; the new Hammett hero was a self-

indulgent playboy who just wanted to be left alone with Nora and her dollars, who came out of retirement to solve the case of the missing thin man only because his wife insisted. What, on the surface, is amusing and fresh in the published version simply reflects Hammett's own decay as an individual and as a writer. The discipline which held him to the typewriter was largely gone; the drinking was constant; the man could no longer believe in, nor write about, detectives who resisted life's pleasures to get a case solved. Nick Charles is, in many ways, an unattractive character—made attractive only by Hammett's wit and clever style. This novel reflects the author's own uncertainty in his career; it foreshadowed the long years of creative silence ahead: after *The Thin Man* just three new short stories appeared (all in 1934).

Hammett's play was never produced, his future novels were never finished. There would be film, radio, and newspaper work, but—at the age of thirty-nine—solid creative prose was behind him. Hammett was never able to shake himself free of the "good life" long enough to create important work; the essential core was gone. Only the hollow man remained.

Dashiell Hammett had written creative prose for twelve years; he would live another two and a half decades as a silent novelist. The humor in *The Thin Man*, looked at in retrospect, is sinister indeed. It is, literally, laughter in the graveyard.

9

FROM A SYNDICATED STRIP TO A DINNER WITH STEIN

IN THE SLICK-PAPER MAGAZINES of the early Thirties Dashiell Hammett was still a current name, and some shorter work, written prior to *The Thin Man,* received major attention. "Woman in the Dark" appeared as a three-part serial in *Liberty,* hailed in a cover blurb as "a new novel of dangerous romance." The story was actually no more than a 15,000-word novelet, but the editor wanted to exploit it as much as possible. One of the nation's top artists, James Montgomery Flagg, was hired to illustrate the "novel," and Hammett's Hollywood agent parlayed the property into a film sale.

In 1934 RKO Radio released "Woman in the Dark," starring Fay Wray, Ralph Bellamy, and Melvyn Douglas. A trio of other writers worked on the screen adaptation, but source credit went to Hammett, and his name was prominently displayed on theater-lobby posters.

One critic dubbed it "strong stuff . . . a typical Hammett crook-cop yarn."

Then, too, the brand new men's magazine, *Esquire,* got not only Ernest Hemingway but Dashiel Hammett for its first (August, 1933) issue. Hammett's contribution was a clever crime short-short, "Albert Pastor at Home."

But Hammett was moving away from prose, and by

late 1933 was engaged in the creation of an original crime-adventure comic strip, "Secret Agent X-9."

Four years earlier two important strips had appeared, "Tarzan" by Harold Foster (based on the Burroughs character) and "Buck Rogers" by Dick Calkins. The humorous comic strip had thus moved into the "illustrated suspense story" category. And with "Dick Tracy," in 1931, the first successful syndicated detective strip appeared, written and drawn by Chester Gould. When King Features approached Hammett to create and write a new adventure series, in competition to "Tracy," they offered substantial money, as well as "a free creative hand," and Hammett agreed to undertake the assignment.

"Secret Agent X-9" made its debut, as a daily strip, in January of 1934. Alex Raymond, soon to achieve fame for his superbly creative "Flash Gordon," was chosen by King Features as Hammett's illustrator. Raymond used a style of action drawing which echoed the pulp magazine school of art, and his characters wore clothing in keeping with the period. The natty X-9 was outfitted in trenchcoat and snap-brim, a silk smoking jacket, or a neat, double-breasted suit, as occasion demanded. Raymond's hoods sported derbies and spats, striped shirts and straw boaters, and his gang molls flounced about in gaudy flapper attire.

Hammett kept the action brisk. The opening adventure (which ran daily for eight months) was full of gun fights, car crashes, gold shipments, piracy, explosions at sea, mysterious code messages, and blackout murders.

Hammett combined the Op and Sam Spade in the character of X-9. He was cool, efficient, quick with a gun or a wisecrack and, like the Op, was a man without a name.

French critic Maurice Horn comments on the "violence and pessimism" in Hammett's creation, dubbing it the first "black" comic strip: "X-9 is an FBI agent. In his struggle against crime, he is not satisfied merely to fight criminals; he mingles with them, borrows their habits,

jargon, and even their methods. . . . The fact that he possesses no known name, only a number, and that he always works alone, further heightens his mystery."

Ron Goulart, also an authority on the comics, finds in this first X-9 "characterizations which are part *Falcon*, part *Dain Curse*, and part *Thin Man* . . . with a good innocent blonde in trouble, a doublecrossing older woman who continually lies, a wacky professor who keeps disappearing, a fat con man named Sidney George Harper Carp who talks like Casper Gutman, and a gang of hoods who kidnap the blonde."

The hoods are Hammett-tough ("You're liable to get slapped around whether you behave yourself or not!"), and the gun molls are equally potent. One of them visits a society woman and clips her smartly on the jaw, knocking her to the floor. "You'll pay for this!" says the victim. "OK, Baby, and you can put this on my bill, too!" replies the snarling young woman, kicking her in the stomach.

X-9 was a hard character. In the second 1934 adventure he is hit over the head, placed in a tunnel of burning oil, survives an auto crash, is blackjacked, and has his parachute fired upon as he jumps out of a plane after the villain. By the third adventure (into March of 1935) he is thrown off a cliff and almost drowned, spending much of the time with one arm in a sling. He once killed four men in four panels, and had no use for sentiment.

When Mel Graff took over the strip in 1939, he softened this hard image. "X-9 was *never* a warm character," Graff stated. "You were supposed to like him because he wore a badge and carried a gun. He never fell in love. I'm changing all that. I've got him engaged to his steno-secretary . . . and I've given the guy a name. He will be known as Phil Corrigan from here on."

Thus, Hammett's X-9 expired and Graff's Phil Corrigan was born.

Later Sam Spade also appeared in a comic-strip format,

but Hammett had nothing to do with this Wildroot Cream Oil version of his detective; he merely collected royalties.

Neither did Hammett write the screenplay for MGM's film, "The Thin Man," but he was on the set during much of the production, and may well have added lines and sequences during the shooting. When the book was first offered for sale the studio was unsure of just what to do with it. Producer Hunt Stromberg brought it to W. S. "Woody" Van Dyke, suggesting that it might be just the vehicle for this action director.

"Woody, if you'll make the picture, I'll buy the story." Van Dyke read it, said yes, and the deal was arranged.

Bosley Crowther, writing in *The Lion's Share*, revealed that "Mayer thought Van Dyke slightly daffy when he asked if he could do a lighthearted, sophisticated mystery thriller with Myrna Loy and Bill Powell. Both people, Mayer said, were 'heavies.' They wouldn't go in comedy. Van Dyke insisted that they could both be droll, and that Miss Loy [who over several years had gravitated from boudoirs to opium dens] if scrubbed up and dressed properly, could be a typical, well-bred American wife. . . . The idea was that the couple should be wholesome and debonair while engaged in the perilous business of catching criminals."

And, after all, hadn't Powell been a hit as Philo Vance?

Mayer finally agreed to let Stromberg and Van Dyke go ahead, "if you can make it quick and cheap."

"I shot it in sixteen days, retakes and all," Van Dyke recalled. "And that sweet smell of success was in every frame."

Albert Hackett and Frances Goodrich did the screenplay, and they were to write two more of the five film sequels, extending into 1947 and starring the popular Powell and Loy team. Hammett created and wrote "original stories" (screen treatments) as the basis for the next two in the

series: "After the Thin Man" (1936) and "Another Thin Man" (1939).

In "After the Thin Man," Nick and Nora go home to San Francisco, where "all the mugs in town" greet Nick warmly. Part of the action takes place in Chinatown, and the plot is a cross mixture of disappearing husbands, a strangling, a dead janitor, blackmail, and a gunman named Dancer who fires at Nick.

Powell and Loy were not the stars of the regular radio series, but they did appear in their original screen roles on The Lux Radio Theater's presentation of "The Thin Man" in June of 1936, making a return appearance on that show for "After the Thin Man" four years later.

Hammett's first Nick Charles film launched a trend in Hollywood. Following the success of "The Thin Man," several "Mr. and Mrs." detective films were produced, yet none captured what one critic called "the wacky, semi-alcoholic appeal of the Charles marriage."

Hammett's last three short stories appeared in *Collier's* early in 1934, and the final one of these, "This Little Pig," deals with Hollywood. In it, the author creates a hack screen writer, one Chauncey "Bugs" Parish, who interrupts a play in progress to heed a producer's frenzied request to "go sex up my Western." Parish finds, on location, intense jealousy among the female actresses, centered around a young starlet, Kitty Doran, who yearns for a larger part in the film. Parish writes her into the picture to teach her a lesson, knowing the leading lady will later make certain the scenes end on the cutting room floor—but after this occurs Kitty apparently tries to kill herself, and Parish rushes to her side, stricken with conscience over his "game." Another actress, who knows the girl is faking, exposes the suicide attempt, and Parish, his cynicism restored, goes off with this actress, leaving a furious Kitty to work her wiles elsewhere. The "little pig" of the title has been too greedy. The

story finds Parish a hack to the end, as he accepts another quickie assignment: "Max Rhinewien had bought a Hungarian comedy which he said needed more epigrams and talked me into doing the adaptation."

In flavor, mood and general structure, this story is much like F. Scott Fitzgerald's Pat Hobby tales, which appeared several years later in *Esquire*. And since Fitzgerald knew and read Hammett it is possible that Hobby might have been partially inspired by Bugs Parish.

"His Brother's Keeper" and "Two Sharp Knives," were also printed in *Collier's* that year. Ellery Queen rated the first of these very highly, calling it "one of Hammett's finest studies of character and background." The story is told in the first person by an eighteen-year-old boxer, Eddie Bolan, whose brother, Loney, sets him up for a fall in the ring, then decides, at the last moment, to let Eddie win. This doublecross costs Loney his life. With this story, Hammett took the reader into the mind of an unschooled, teenage boxer. Yet, for all of its narrative power, "His Brother's Keeper" fails in plotting; it is smooth, slick, and thin.

"Two Sharp Knives" is an understated crime tale, narrated by police chief Scott Anderson, whose trusted officer, Wally Shane, is revealed as the murderer. Terse and direct, it has a stronger plot and is superior to the boxing story.

When Gertrude Stein came to California in 1935, she declared that there were only two American men she wanted to meet: Charles Chaplin and Dashiell Hammett. A dinner party was arranged in Beverly Hills, Chaplin and Hammett attending with Paulette Goddard, Anita Loos, and other guests. Lillian Hellman accompanied Hammett, and reports that "Miss Stein told Dash he was the only American writer who wrote well about women." Hammett looked pleased. He smiled, pointing to Lillian as his source.

Ironically, there was a dramatic reversal in the careers of Hammett and Lillian Hellman. Just as 1934 marked the end of Hammett's completed creative fiction, it also marked the beginning of Lillian Hellman's success as a playwright. By the close of that year, her first staged drama, "The Children's Hour," was a triumph in New York, *Vanity Fair* calling it "one of the most literate, sensitive, and human dramas in the contemporary theater."

"The Children's Hour" was based on a true law case which Hammett brought to Lillian Hellman's attention, giving her "a solid foundation to build on." The case concerned a pair of old-maid school teachers in nineteenth-century Edinburgh whose private school was wrecked, along with their reputations, when unjust charges of lesbianism were brought against them by one of their students. Hammett thought this case would make a fine basis for a stage drama, and Hellman wrote it, redoing the entire play at least six times, writing some scenes as many as twenty times, before she and Hammett were satisfied. (She later adapted "The Children's Hour" as a film for Samuel Goldwyn and United Artists in 1936, under the title "These Three.")

Lillian Hellman was news. One reporter described her as "five feet three inches tall, slim, with reddish hair, a fine, aquiline nose and a level, humorous mouth." Another early interviewer was not so flattering: "She's the kind of girl who can take the tops off bottles with her teeth." Which must have amused Hammett; he liked strong women.

10

POLITICS, FAULKNER, AND A CLASSIC FALCON

SCREEN PROJECTS CONTINUED to occupy Dashiell Hammett during 1935. His agent kept him busy with "patch jobs," which involved his going in during the production of a film and writing last-minute scenes and emergency dialogue, work which was always uncredited but lucrative. Although, in Hollywood terms, this was "hacking," it is well known that both F. Scott Fitzgerald and Ben Hecht (among others) worked without credit in patching "Gone With the Wind," and William Faulkner, who was officially credited as the writer on six films, actually worked on forty-four.

Two more Hammett pictures were released in 1935, "The Glass Key" and "Mister Dynamite." The former was produced by Paramount, and despite the fact that Hammett remained away from the project, his exact dialogue was often utilized from the novel, particularly in the scenes with the apelike Jeff, chillingly played by Guinn Williams. These scenes were very faithful to the book, but the basic man-woman climax was dropped by the scriptors. (In 1942, when Paramount remade the story, Hammett's original ending was restored.)

Hammett's second film that year, "Mister Dynamite," was based on an original screen treatment he wrote for Universal. It dealt with a Spade-like private eye in San

Francisco (named Dynamite) who tangles with local authority in his pursuit of the killer. The film was reviewed as "a comedy with homicidal interruptions."

Warner Brothers tried again with *The Maltese Falcon* in 1936, using Bette Davis as star, and changing the entire plot and characters. Hefty Alison Skipworth played a *female* Gutman; Warren William was the detective (called Ted Shayne in this version); Brown Holmes wrote a screenplay which replaced the Falcon with a jeweled French horn. The private eye ended up marrying his secretary in this uncertain production which went through several prerelease titles from "Men on Her Mind" to "Hard Luck Dame." The final: "Satan Met a Lady." As directed by William Dieterle, the picture was justly termed "nonsensical" and fizzled at the box-office. Hammett's credit line, "from a story by" did not carry the title of his original novel.

Hammett's dealings with producers were often erratic, and columnist Leonard Lyons recalled the time the author met producer Dudley Murphy at the 21 Club. "Murphy scrawled out a contract on the back of a menu," says Lyons. "The next year Dash wrote to Murphy asking for a similar deal on a new story—and enclosed a fresh 21 Club menu!"

Another producer with an "ideal" property for Hammett to adapt made an appointment to see the author when Hammett was occupying a suite at the Beverly-Wilshire. The producer was shown into the main living room by a houseboy and told to wait. He waited. And waited. Finally, the inner study door slowly opened and Hammett appeared there in a silk lounging robe, a scarf at his neck, a drink in his hand. He stood unmoving, cool-eyed, silent.

The producer began his pitch, gesturing, pacing the room, presenting his ideas enthusiastically for several minutes. At the conclusion of the pitch Hammett was totally silent. The silence lengthened. Then Hammett said one word, "No," turned abruptly and closed the door behind

him. The producer was shown out by the houseboy.

Hammett's independent attitude toward studio heads amused Raymond Chandler. "He was one of the many guys who couldn't take Hollywood without trying to push God out of the high seat," wrote Chandler in 1945. "We only met once, at a *Black Mask* dinner in the Thirties . . . but I liked him very much."

It was during this period that Hammett began to become politically involved with left-wing causes. He was an ardent anti-fascist, and supported the Loyalists in the Spanish Civil War (as did Hemingway and Hellman, who were both in Madrid during the shelling of that city).

In the summer of 1937 Hemingway's film, "The Spanish Earth," was given a special preview-showing at a pro-Loyalist benefit held in the home of Fredric March in Hollywood, with Hammett, Errol Flynn, Robert Montgomery, and Scott Fitzgerald in attendance. Hemingway was there to pass the hat for his Spanish friends, and several of the guests contributed thousand-dollar checks. (Orson Welles, John Steinbeck, Paul Muni, and Edward G. Robinson also faithfully supported the Loyalists.)

Many writers felt as Hammett felt: disillusioned, cynical, anxious to see changes in corrupt government practices, but few of them remained as stubbornly active over the years. (Steinbeck's political novel, *In Dubious Battle*, appeared in 1936, *The Grapes of Wrath* three years later.)

At least one critic has found weakness, not strength, in this absorption with left-wing politics. David T. Bazelon finds, in Hammett's long "silence" as a writer after the early Thirties, an inability to deal, on a personal level, with "true consciousness—by which I mean a comprehensive hypothesis as to the nature of real life, as opposed to 'a formula.' [This] is either accepted as an essential, growing factor in the structure of one's life, or else it suffers continual distortion—not by accident, but inevitably. . . . Unlike many victims of the Popular Front [the Spanish Loyalist

cause], Hammett went on following the Communists, up hill and down dale: Popular Front—No Front—Second Front."

George P. Elliott, writing in *The Nation,* stated: "Hammett's vision was of a society so corrupt that it corrupts all individual relationships; it is not surprising that he turned to left-wing politics."

And Richard Schickel restated this when he wrote: "Hammett, a leftist, regarded moral evil as economically determined . . . he never tried to supply his heroes with social consciousness [yet he] grew increasingly aware of the distance between the code [doing the job] and his political beliefs. He wrote *The Thin Man,* and then fell silent, unable to bridge the gap."

"Certainly he was a Marxist," declared Lillian Hellman, "but he was a very critical Marxist, often contemptuous of the Soviet Union . . . and often witty and bitingly sharp about the American Communist Party. A great deal about communism worried him."

Beyond politics, hunting exerted a strong appeal in Hammett's life, a passion he shared with William Faulkner, who joined him often during the Thirties for hunting weekends. The two men had much in common: Faulkner admired Hammett's crime fiction just as Hammett admired Faulkner's work; both men enjoyed long conversations; both were strong drinkers; both were from the South; both had written a great deal for Hollywood. (Faulkner's excellent short story, "The Golden Land," is based on his screenwriting sojourns, and he helped adapt Raymond Chandler's classic private eye saga, "The Big Sleep," to the screen. Faulkner hated working in Hollywood, once confessing to a friend that it was "a kind of purgatory, a place where it was necessary to come from time to time to do penance.")

The film world, with its bright, fevered talents, held Dashiell Hammett's attention. He continued to drink and

mingle with the town's crop of creative luminaries: Fitzgerald, Dorothy Parker, King Vidor, Robert E. Sherwood, James Hilton, Perelman, and West.

Yet during that summer of 1937, Hammett settled down to work with Lillian Hellman in an island cottage off South Norwalk as critic and advisor on "The Little Foxes."

Since "Days to Come" had ended as "a harrowing flop," Lillian Hellman was having many problems with "The Little Foxes." Hammett worked painstakingly with her, page by slow page, and was tough and unrelenting in his criticism.

In February of 1939, the opening night party for "Foxes" was held in Baltimore. It was a wildly successful affair. Dorothy Parker argued with Tallulah Bankhead; Sara and Gerald Murphy nostalgically recalled the Riviera antics of Scott and Zelda Fitzgerald; Lillian Hellman experimented with exotic food-and-drink combinations, stirring whiskey sours and dry martinis into a plate of baked Maryland crabmeat, while Hammett conducted what Hellman termed "his usual alcoholic literary discussion" with a confused clerk from the Post Office who had innocently wandered into the party.

Celebration was justified, since this new play was a hit.

In New York, Hammett encountered an old friend, Orson Welles, who asked him if he knew of anyone who would be willing to invest some instant money in "Five Kings," a Shakespearian project foundering for lack of funds. Welles told Hammett that he desperately needed fifteen thousand dollars to save the production.

A meeting was arranged between Welles and a Texas millionaire who was, according to Hammett, "very anxious" to finance important theatrical properties.

"Just leave everything to me," Hammett told him. "Now let's have a drink." They had several.

The next morning Hammett marched Welles into the Plaza Hotel to meet the Texan, and mellowed by a long

night of alcoholic pleasure, hailed the prospective backer with the ill-chosen phrase, "Hello, sucker!"

That did it.

This greeting, Welles later reflected, cost him seven thousand five hundred dollars a word.

Hammett returned to Hollywood for more routine film assignments, and by mid-September of 1940 Scott Fitzgerald was referring to him as "a spoiled writer." In a letter to Gerald Murphy, Fitzgerald (then only three months away from death) talked of Hollywood as "a slack, soft place" and named those he called "the spoiled writers, Hecht, Nunnally Johnson, Dotty [Parker], Dashiell Hammett . . ."

Yet Hammett's name continued to command attention. Another of his "Thin Man" films had been released; he had appeared in Ellery Queen's first anthology with a Sam Spade reprint; Orson Welles had adapted his *Glass Key* to radio; he'd helped found and shape the liberal publication, *PM,* in New York City. By the Fall of 1941, with the first issue of *Ellery Queen's Mystery Magazine,* Frederic Dannay and Manfred B. Lee began to resurrect Hammett's early pulp tales for reprinting in their new publication. And Howard Haycraft devoted six pages to Hammett as a "master" of the art of the detective story in *Murder For Pleasure*: "They [his novels] established new standards of realism in the genre. . . . Commercial in conception, they miss being Literature, if at all, by the narrowest of margins. . . ." Haycraft mentioned Hammett's "ability to delineate character by sharp, frugal, telling strokes admirably suited to the form . . . the prose is economical, astringent and muscular. . . . Hammett's lean, dynamic, unsentimental narratives created a definitely *American* style, quite separate and distinct from the accepted English pattern . . . and no other author of modern times—certainly no other American—has so basically changed and influenced the form . . . he has given the American detective story a nationality of its own."

Yet the biggest "popular advance" for Hammett during 1941 came with the release of John Huston's version of "The Maltese Falcon." In his comprehensive anthology (co-edited with Laura Kerr), *Hello Hollywood!*, screen writer Allen Rivkin tells an amusing story of how the novel came to be filmed for the third time.

John Huston (who wanted to be a film director, and who had already directed his father, actor Walter Huston, on the New York stage the previous year) wanted Rivkin to collaborate on a screen version of *Falcon*. "Warner said if I can get a good screenplay out of this Dash Hammett thing, he'll let me direct." Rivkin read it, liked it, agreed to help Huston. "Fine," Huston told him. "Have the secretary recopy the book, just setting it up in basic shots, scenes, dialogue. We'll start from there."

The secretary did as instructed, says Rivkin, and her copy fell into the hands of studio head Jack Warner, who was delighted with the manner in which the novel had been "adapted." He phoned Huston and told him to shoot it that way. John was amazed, but happily accepted. "I was out of a job!" Rivkin stated, echoing Huston's declaration that it was "the god-damndest thing!"

Huston did some cutting and minor touch-up on the "script" before going into production, but it was almost entirely Hammett's novel. "Hammett remains the real author of the film without ever having worked on it," wrote critic Allen Eyles. "Huston . . . imposed no viewpoint of his own, but sought to realize on film the atmosphere of the book, merging precisely into the aloof position Hammett adopts in his writing. Hammett's style is tersely descriptive, involving no explanations of any of his characters, and is entirely concerned in conveying a situation by its externals, letting events speak for themselves."

Although the film retains the novel's dialogue, almost word for word, there *are* deletions. Huston eliminated a minor character (Gutman's daughter) and dropped the Flit-

craft parable; he also toned down the homosexual aspects of the Cairo-Cook relationship. And Huston's sharp ear for dialogue improved the exchange between Cairo and Spade, when the former offers a retaining fee. "You will take, say, one hundred dollars?" he asks, and Spade replies (in the novel), "Better make it two hundred." Huston's line was sharper: "I will take, say, two hundred." And then there's the detective's final reply, as he holds the phony lead falcon, and one of the cops asks what it is. Bogart coolly delivers the line: "The stuff that dreams are made of."

Bogart was the ideal Sam Spade. Yet, had George Raft said yes to Jack Warner, he would have been cast in the role. Raft, who had also turned down the Bogart role in "High Sierra," felt that he did not wish to entrust his talents to Huston, an untested writer-turned-director, with a property that had twice bombed at the box-office.

Bogie was forty-two; he'd been around a long while, having made his first film in 1930, and was just weathered enough and tough enough to look the part of Spade (one critic remarking on ". . . that face that seems to have been eroded and battered by harsh words and blunt instruments").

Paced by Bogart, the cast was perfection itself.

Mary Astor (born in 1906 as Lucille Langehanke) was superb as Brigid O'Shaughnessy, projecting just the proper blend of sensuality and false innocence. At sixty-one, weighing in at 285, actor Sydney Greenstreet was picked by Huston from the New York stage to portray the oily Casper Gutman. He had been acting since 1904, playing Broadway comedy for three decades; this was his first film. Peter Lorre (real name Lazlo Lowenstein) was shrewdly chosen for the perfumed rogue, Cairo. (Lorre became a close friend to Bogart—and appeared with Greenstreet in seven more films after "Falcon.") Wilmer, the boy gunsel, was nastily acted by Elisha Cook, soft-faced, yet properly menacing.

Even the supporting players were perfectly cast—and

each became memorable: Barton MacLane as Dundy, the tough cop; Ward Bond as Polhaus; Jerome Cowan as Spade's doomed partner, Miles Archer; Lee Patrick as the faithful Effie; quavery Gladys George as Archer's widow, Iva.

John's father, Walter Huston, accepted an uncredited bit part "for luck" in his son's first cinema effort. The elder Huston played the mortally wounded Captain Jacobi, who staggers into Spade's office, drops the falcon, and expires. (Imitating the voice of the picture's producer, Hal Wallis, John phoned his father the evening after this scene had been shot, and told him he was "terrible" in it, that he had "chewed up the scenery" and that he must come back the next morning and re-do the scene. Walter Huston was furious, but agreed to the retake, having fallen for his son's practical joke. John twitted him about it for years.)

Jack Warner wanted to call the finished film "The Gent from Frisco," explaining to Huston that the original title of the novel had already been used. "Aw, hell, Jack," Huston muttered, "nobody will remember that dog." And he was right.

Production was completed in two months, at a total cost of $300,000. Hammett got no additional money, but the final satisfaction was his.

London's *Sunday Times* named "Falcon" as "the most interesting and imaginative detective film to come out of America—or anywhere else—since the first 'Thin Man.' It is, of course, not irrelevant that both stories have the same author, Dashiell Hammett."

"Huston follows Hammett faithfully," wrote critic Eugene Archer, "recording his exact dialogue and even following the author's directions for movements and gestures . . . and Huston's sense of humor and irony clearly parallels Hammett's at every point. . . . The result is a completely faithful cinematic transcription of a novel, with a singleness of purpose which adds to its force."

Alan S. Downer, in *Man and the Movies,* calls this third film version of the book "possibly the most successful screen realization of a novel ever achieved."

Shortly after the release of the Huston version, Warner Brothers announced a sequel, "The Further Adventures of the Maltese Falcon," which Huston was to write and direct with his original cast, but this never jelled. Yet there was one more "Maltese Falcon"—with Edward G. Robinson as Spade. This was aired early in 1943 by the Lux Radio Theater, and Gail Patrick played Brigid to Laird Cregar's Gutman. Three years later Hammett's tough detective would emerge as a popular radio hero played by Howard Duff.

Sam Spade had become a part of American folklore.

11

WAR AND THE DARKER MOOD

DURING THE SUMMER PRECEDING Pearl Harbor, with America on the edge of World War II, Hammett worked with Lillian Hellman at her 130-acre farm in Pleasantville, New York. The task: a screen adaptation of her award-winning stage drama, "Watch on the Rhine." Hammett had great respect for the play, and wanted to be as faithful to it as Huston had been to his novel.

"Watch on the Rhine" became Hammett's only solo screenplay, but he claimed no credit for the job. "The material was all there," he declared. "I simply arranged it in screen form." When the picture was released the New York *Herald Tribune* commented: "Dashiell Hammett, who did the screenplay . . . has retained practically every word . . . adding only a few scenes because of the wider latitude of the screen."

Hammett's screenplay was eventually honored with inclusion in the *Best Film Plays* series. It was to be his last direct contribution to Hollywood.

He now became active in radio.

The Thin Man had been sold to NBC in 1942, and Hammett worked on a number of the early scripts to help launch the radio series. Lestor Damon played Nick Charles and Claudia Morgan was Nora. Himan Brown produced and directed.

"The Thin Man and the Flack," one of Hammett's 1942 radio scripts, was "scenarized" for *Click* magazine that season, in a photo-and-caption-story format. The style is tough-funny, on the direct, unsubtle level of the X-9 strip: "I was minding my own business, my own wife, and my own drink at Barney's. Al Thornton was sitting at the next table with Sonia Bellkoff, the Russian lollypop Monarch signed up. Al was Sonia's flack." It seems Miss Bellkoff is in "a hell of a jam," and seeks Nick's help. In the midst of her story "a barking pistol cut her short." The shot, however, turns out to be a blank, a flack's publicity stunt. Later, Nick gets another call. This time Sonia is really shot—mortally. A pistol is brandished. ("I jumped him. After I took his gun away I poured myself a nice stiff drink.") Nick has the killer: Al. No stunt this time. Jealousy, over a broken promise.

Well below par for Hammett, but entertaining enough for a popular radio show. And the pay was excellent.

By September, 1942, Hammett was garnering publicity as president of the Writers League of America, which strongly favored a Second Front. Criticism, from several sources, was leveled at Hammett; he was making political enemies, some of whom accused him of being an enemy of America.

Yet that same month, on September 19, he confounded his critics and amazed his friends by joining the U.S. Army Signal Corps at the age of forty-eight.

"Dash failed his physical exam at Camp Upton, New York," says a friend. "The reason the doctors gave him was rotten teeth. So he went out and had them pulled. When he returned they had to induct him."

A serviceman who shared Hammett's quarters in the early stages of his training was surprised when the man they were calling "Pop" volunteered for overseas service. "He had a good deal going for himself at Fort Monmouth, New Jersey—where he was assigned as a Signal Corps instructor,

but he said he wanted to see some action. I guess it had something to do with his personal campaign to fight fascism."

Whatever his reasons, Cpl. S. D. Hammett was granted an overseas post—and was shipped to remote, storm-blasted Adak, at the tip of the Aleutians in the Pacific. Stretching west for a thousand miles, the Aleutian Islands were formed from the tops of submerged mountain peaks, an extension of the rugged volcanic ranges of the Alaskan Peninsula. Liberator bombers bounded into the air off Adak's choppy landing strip to attack enemy-held Attu and Kiska. (John Huston, who arrived on Adak just ahead of Hammett, filmed his famous documentary, "Report From the Aleutians," in this same area.)

Hammett wrote of the Willawaw, "the sudden wild wind of the Islands," and of the "black Aleutian mud," and of 110-mile-an-hour gusts of rain squalls from Siberia, but he really didn't mind the weather or the locale. It stimulated him; he maintained a good humor with the troops, "playing it straight and asking no favors."

Shortly after he had arrived on Adak the commanding general asked him to do the men a favor. "They need a daily newspaper out here. You're a writer. You edit it."

Hammett complained that he'd entered the service to get away from writing, but the general was insistent. How many men would he need for the job? Hammett told him ten. He got them.

"The paper was published at night," reports a sergeant who served with Hammett. "Pop usually got out of the sack around 9 P.M., worked all night, went back to bed around 6 A.M. Every day we got four pages of world news, cartoons, jokes—and occasional editorials by Pop himself. He wrote real fine."

Hammett spent a year and a half on Adak, and liked the place. "The trouble is, the men here walk with their heads down. They don't lift their heads up long enough to

see how beautiful the islands are . . . there's little difference between winter and summer here. In the winter, you've got snow up to your waist; in the summer, there's mud up to your waist. But you get used to it."

Most GIs didn't. Complained one, "You had to crawl to the latrines because if you stood up the wind would take you to Siberia." Hammett often set out on long walks across the mountains ringing the area, wind whipping his white hair, his long, gaunt frame bent against the gale-force, enjoying himself thoroughly. "My health is improving here," he declared.

By 1944 he was on Kiska, the Japanese having withdrawn after heavy losses. Hammett later recalled the "crazy major" who wanted him to go into cattle-raising in the Aleutians after the war ended. Before he was transferred, Hammett worked on a battle history of the islands with Cpl. Robert Colodny, completing it a year after his arrival on Kiska. *The Battle of the Aleutians* (sub-titled: *A Graphic History: 1942–1943*) ran to 4,000 words of text with captioned drawings and maps. The twenty-four-page pamphlet, an illustrated campaign history of the first two years of fighting, was produced by the Intelligence Section, Field Force Headquarters on Adak, and bore Hammett's name as co-writer. It was never commercially released.

During his service in the Aleutians, Hammett became something of a legend with the troops, who saw in this crag-faced man who'd lived half a century a certain strength they could admire, a maturity to respect. The story is told of the time several of Hammett's bunk-mates were moaning over their womanless existence. Hammett listened patiently, then said, "Look, a woman *would* be nice, but not getting any doesn't cause your teeth or hair to fall out . . . and if you kiddies don't stop this stuff I'm going to move."

They shut up. ("We didn't want to lose him!")

Hammett enjoyed his role as "Pop," lending the boys money, paying their bar bills, sending one of them on mar-

riage leave with enough extra cash for the honeymoon. As in the palmy days of Hollywood, he spent money quickly, emotionally; it could bring pleasure, and he used it that way.

Promoted to the rank of sergeant, Hammett was sent to Anchorage, Alaska, where he was assigned to the Information and Education section. He spent the last six months of his duty there, editing a monthly publication for the department.

"Pop never went to movies in the service," recalls an overseas buddy. "You'd think, him being a screen writer and all, he'd have gone to plenty of them. But he just went to one, a picture called 'Watch on the Rhine.' "

Hammett was amused by a question he was constantly asked in those days: why had he turned down a commission? ("I always had to explain that no one had ever offered me one.")

In August of 1945 he was moved to Edmonton, Alberta, on temporary duty. Headlines announced his arrival. Once more he was Dashiell Hammett, the famous writer. Was Mr. Hammett going to do a novel based on his experiences in the Aleutians? No, Mr. Hammett was not. Mr. Hammett was going to do a book about a guy who comes home and doesn't like his family.

By September he had left the service and was back in civilian tweeds, declaring that the Army was "the steadiest job I ever had."

He was fifty-one.

He had contracted emphysema.

He would never be entirely well again for the remainder of his life.

Back home, Hammett discovered that he had been hailed as the mystery story's "ace performer" by Raymond Chandler in an *Atlantic* essay. Additionally, three more of his paperback collections were out: *The Adventures of Sam Spade, The Continental Op* and *The Return of the*

Continental Op, all published by Lawrence E. Spivak and edited by Ellery Queen. (The Spade collection also appeared in hard covers from World.)

The Continental Op contained four Op tales, beginning with "Fly Paper," which Hammett had written in 1929. Two others were from his 1924 period, the last from 1930. *The Return of the Continental Op* contained five; two novelets from 1925, the last Op story ("Death and Company") from 1930, and a pair from 1924. These nine stories, untouched by Hammett from magazine to book, held up as hard, stripped examples of what was now called "the Hammett School." They had not dated. Ellery Queen, in an introduction to the stories, praised Hammett as "without question one of the great writers of mystery fiction, and the leader in our generation."

But the man behind the words was restive once again. The war no longer occupied him; he could not "get moving" on his novel or his play; film writing was behind him. Hammett began to repeat the drinking pattern that had plagued him in Hollywood and New York.

In late November of 1945 he received a letter from his old *Black Mask* editor, Joe Shaw. The letter began, ironically, by remarking on the fact that Shaw had heard "in what fine shape you have come out of the Army." Shaw then mentioned that he had been responsible for Spivak's 1943 publication of *Blood Money* and that the response to this book was such that "Spivak had me dig out all of your earlier stories." Then Shaw got to the point: he wanted permission from Hammett to include one of his stories in a *Black Mask* anthology he was editing for Simon and Schuster. He told Hammett the publisher wanted him to use "The Big Knockover," as a separate novelet, and would that be all right? The fee was $100 for use of the story in a book then tentatively titled *A Treasury of Early Black Mask Stories*, a volume which finally emerged as *The Hard-Boiled Omnibus*.

Hammet said no, that the money was not sufficient to cover such a long story. How about a shorter one for the same fee? Shaw agreed, considered using "The Main Death," then decided on "Fly Paper," which became the only story in the book representing the Twenties. The other eleven dated from 1930 into 1936. (Shaw had been replaced as editor of *Black Mask* late in 1936.)

An examination of Shaw's correspondence relating to this anthology reveals that he very much wanted to include Erle Stanley Gardner in the volume.

Gardner turned Shaw down, declaring that he did not think editor Phil Cody was getting the credit he deserved in the formation of the *Black Mask* style of writing.

"Cody was the first man to appreciate the real genius of Dashiell Hammett," Gardner declared, "and he was editor during the period when Hammett developed his Continental Op." Gardner would not allow his work to appear in a collection which made it seem as if *Black Mask* had achieved its style exclusively under Shaw's editorship.

Upset by this, Shaw wrote a defensive letter to Gardner's agent, Willis Wing, in which he stated: "It was only when Hammett began to set character before situation, and led some others along that path, did he in any way attain recognition. This change, as can readily be seen by an examination of his republished stories, shall I say, chanced to happen shortly after I came to the magazine in 1926."

Although Shaw greatly encouraged Hammett, and drew from him the major novels on which his reputation stands, the fact remains that as early as 1924, with a story such as "The Man Who Killed Dan Odams," Hammett was very definitely placing "character before situation." The well-characterized "Zigzags of Treachery" was printed in 1924, as was "The Girl With the Silver Eyes." And 1925 saw such Hammett stories in print as "The Whosis Kid" and "Dead Yellow Women." Shaw's statement, therefore,

was not a valid one, yet his influence in the later *Black Mask* years cannot be denied.

The editor's introductory remarks in *The Hard-Boiled Omnibus* amplify his basic idea that *Black Mask*, under his guidance, was "a unique magazine and a new influence in American literature." Shaw speaks of the development of the "hard, brittle style" he wanted in *Black Mask*. "These writers observed the cardinal principle in creating the illusion of reality: they did not *make* their characters act and talk tough; they *allowed* them to . . . their product . . . was several years ahead of its time."

During the summer of 1946, while Hammett's name was being connected with the Civil Rights Congress, radio's William Spier contacted Wildroot Cream Oil with a series idea. Spier had seen Hammett's book, *The Adventures of Sam Spade,* and felt that it was an excellent basis for a radio show, under the same title. Would Wildroot sponsor the project? They said yes, but who would play Sam Spade?

Many actors were tested and rejected. "I'm after a certain tough quality of voice which is either there or it isn't," Spier declared. "I'll know it when I hear it."

When he heard the voice of Howard Duff, Spier knew he had the right man. Duff was signed, and Lurene Tuttle became Effie. Spier directed the show, which made its debut in the fall of 1946.

The announcer's opening was delivered in the crisp style of a news bulletin: "Dashiell Hammett, America's leading detective fiction writer and creator of Sam Spade, the hard-boiled private eye, and William Spier, radio's outstanding director of mystery and crime drama, join their talents to make your hair stand on end with 'The Adventures of Sam Spade' . . . presented by Wildroot Cream Oil!"

Actually, Hammett did join his talent with that of Spier, and wrote several scripts for the show. In one two-part episode he brought back Casper Gutman and Joel

Cairo, with a new gunsel, in a search for a unique treasure, the Kandy Tooth. This tooth, from the mouth of a jeweled Buddha, set off a chase to America, in which the treasure is finally destroyed. It had been installed in the bridgework of a "carrier" in order to smuggle it out of India, but the man was cremated, tooth and all, before Gutman could reach him. As with the falcon from Malta, the fat man had been cheated once again of his prize.

The series was extremely popular. Duff was cocky, hard, wise, and humorous as Spade—but he was not Bogart and he was not the Spade of Hammett's novel. Spier kept the touch light, used the wisecrack as Spade's trademark. This became apparent shortly after Hammett quit writing for the series. Radio historian Jim Harmon remarked on this: "The show was outright satire, played not so much for drama as for comedy. . . . The scripts by Bob Tallman and Gil Doud were clearly wild parodies of the taut, often grim Hammett work of the Thirties."

During that same year, 1946, Hammett developed and sold another radio series, "The Fat Man." The new series did not deal, as one might suppose, with Casper Gutman, but with a crime hunter named Brad Runyon (played by a real fat man, J. Scott Smart). Robert Sloane wrote most of the segments—and a film, starring Smart, was made from the series in 1951 by Universal, using the show's original title. (Hammett received no official screen credit on this story, reported by the local trades as "taken from the Dashiell Hammett private eye character.")

"After Hammett's first few scripts 'setting' the series," states Jim Harmon, "the radio program sank into pedestrian mediocrity . . . he had fared better with 'The Thin Man' series as a generally reliable pastiche of his work, than with 'The Fat Man,' which became a poor imitation."

Hammett never concerned himself with the quality of his radio shows beyond the point when he stopped being personally involved in them; they paid well and people lis-

tened to them. They were serving their purpose. They were not, could never be, fully creative in the sense of a novel or a play.

In response to heavy reader demand, Ellery Queen edited another collection of the author's early fiction, *Hammett Homicides,* which appeared in December, 1946. In this edition Queen printed the two related "Silver Eyes" novelets from 1924, a short from the same year, and another from 1927. Added to these Op adventures were "Two Sharp Knives" from *Collier's* (1934) and "Ruffian's Wife" from *Sunset* (1925). Queen's original plan for a Hammett trilogy was now, he announced, expanded to a pentalogy. The fifth, *Dead Yellow Women,* would be out the following year.

In 1947 Hammett was an instructor in creative writing at the Jefferson School of Social Science in New York. He was also working on his play, but keeping it well away from prying eyes. Its tentative title, "The Summer Meal," its subject matter, "people." Hammett would say no more.

Drinking remained a severe and desperate problem. One of Hammett's students at the school recalls that "he'd come in glassy-eyed, his hair all tangled, looking pretty bad. It was obvious he'd been hitting the bottle before class. But he pulled himself together for us. He taught us that tempo is the vital thing in fiction, that you've got to keep things moving, that character can be drawn within the action rather than outside it. He was very serious, very intense when he talked about writing."

Dead Yellow Women contained, in addition to the superb title novelet from 1925, two more *Black Mask* Op tales, one from 1923, another from 1924. Additionally, Hammett's one Op story from *True Detective* in 1924, "Who Killed Bob Teal?" was also there, along with two early non-Op stories. A special passage in "Who Killed Bob Teal?" which Hammett had put into the manuscript to satisfy the editor was retained for this first book printing of

the story: "Those who remember this affair," says the Op, "will know that the city, the detective agency, and the people involved all had names different from the ones I have given them. But they will know also that I have kept the facts true."

Hammett was satisfying the demands of a true-crime magazine when he wrote this passage, yet it is quite possible that the story and its characters, as with many of the Hammett Op pieces, had a solid basis in fact. (The original story, in *True Detective,* was curiously bylined: by Dashiell Hammett, of the Continental Detective Agency.)

The Hammett paperback boom was not over; in February of 1948 another collection appeared, *Nightmare Town,* which contained the 1924 title novelet from *Argosy All-Story,* two Ops from 1925, and the author's 1933 short-short from *Esquire.*

Ellery Queen informed the reader: "This time we say positively 'That's all there is, there isn't any more.' . . . This is the last in our series of Dashiell Hammett short stories."

Of course it was not; three more volumes were due to complete the series.

Aside from the money he received from these collections of early fiction, Hammett remained free of them. He did not revise the work as it went into book form; he saw "no real permanence" in these paperback books.

"This hard-boiled stuff has become a menace," he said, referring to the proliferation of the school he had helped establish; he wanted nothing to do with his past work. It was done, behind him. If Spivak and Queen wanted to dig it up, story by story, then let them; he would happily spend the money they paid him.

In a review of *Nightmare Town,* Anthony Boucher declared that "no writer has suffered more from his imitators than has Hammett. The pygmies have aped his tough terseness without realizing that Hammett told stories of

character, that the key scenes are not the spectacular bloodlettings, but the quiet, tense interplays of character in dialogue."

Alcoholism had now replaced tuberculosis as the disease which ravaged Hammett. He became "lost" in drink, was unable to care for himself, was finally hospitalized.

"If you go on drinking after you leave here," his doctor warned, "you'll be dead in a few months. That's a fact. Now, what are you going to do?"

Hammett regarded him somberly. "I'll quit," he said. "And that's a promise."

The doctor did not believe him. Hammett was too far gone. Too many years of alcoholism had eroded his system, his will. He could never stop drinking.

But he did.

"I gave my word," said Hammett, "and I keep my word when I give it."

12

PRISON AND THE CODE

WITH HIS ALCOHOLIC PROBLEM under control, Hammett resumed hunting, roaming the woods with old friends, using a hearing aid in an experimental attempt to pick up special bird sounds, and trying to get a novel going. He informed his agent that he'd soon have a new book ready. Random House was waiting to publish it, and the title, declared Hammett, was *December 1st.* His collections from Queen continued to appear, with a 1950 edition of *The Creeping Siamese* (a volume containing three Op stories, a crime short and a pair of 1920's *Black Mask* tales). Two other titles, *Woman in the Dark* and *A Man Named Thin,* were announced.

Actually, Hammett was doing far more reading than writing, and would devour almost any book he could lay hands on: books on how to tie knots, on inland birds, chess, the history of the snapping turtle, German gun-makers, the shore life of the Atlantic, true crime, bees, poisonous plants.

"Dash read like most people eat," said a friend. "He chewed up all kinds of books. And he'd absorb them, learn from them. Ask him about the history of Indian religion, or about New Orleans jazz, Greek architecture, glassmaking, baseball, topology. He could talk on any of these subjects."

Hammett spent an entire summer reading about the retina of the eye. He delved into Icelandic sagas, spent a month on the cross-pollination of corn, months on plasma physics, many years on mathematics.

Hammett had never really enjoyed the company of most other writers. Forced to attend a New York cocktail party—in his drinking days—filled with famous names from the publishing world, he would retreat to a far corner with his scotch and stare moodily at the wall. "You'd go over and say hello and introduce yourself and he'd just look up coldly at you," recalled one New York celebrity. "You got the idea he wished you'd drop dead right on the spot. I didn't like the bastard."

Writer Sanora Babb recalls that she "knew Dash for years, at parties, and I don't remember a thing he ever said."

On March 7, 1951, Lillian Hellman's new play, "The Autumn Garden," opened at the Coronet Theater in New York, starring Fredric March and Florence Eldridge. Hammett was there, sweating out the play's debut, since he'd been involved in this production from the beginning. He had contributed one of the key speeches, delivered by a character named Griggs, a retired general.

Griggs speaks of the "turning point" in a life, when you are able to "wipe out your past mistakes, do the work you'd never done, think the way you'd never thought, have what you'd never had . . . ." A man either is ready for the moment, has trained himself for it, or "you've let it all run past you and frittered yourself away." He ends by admitting, "I've frittered myself away."

The speech was a sad one, reflecting defeat, yet it contained great clarity and honesty.

"Dash was hipped on the subject," Hellman said. "The basic idea was his. He worked all night on that speech."

A political crisis was building in Hammett's life. It came to a head in mid-1951, when, as a bail bond fund trustee for the Civil Rights Congress, Hammett was sub-

poenaed for questioning in a case involving four Communists. On trial for conspiracy against the U.S. government, they had jumped bail and disappeared. Hammett and two other bond trustees were asked to name the contributors to the fund.

The night before he was to appear in court, Lillian Hellman asked Hammett to state, simply, that he did not have any names to give. ("The truth was that Hammett had never been in the office of the Committee and did not know the name of a single contributor.")

Hammett refused.

"I hate this damn kind of talk, but maybe I better tell you that if it were more than jail, if it were my life, I would give it for what I think democracy is, and I don't let cops or judges tell me what democracy is."

He had served in two wars, going into the second when most men counted themselves lucky to be out of draft range; he fought when, where and for what he believed. That was his personal code, and he would stick rigidly by it.

Judgment was swift. Convicted of contempt, Hammett was sentenced to serve a six-month term in federal prison. All appeals failed; the sentence was carried out.

On July 10, 1951, he was taken to New York's West Street jail, then moved to a federal penitentiary in West Virginia, and later (in September) to a prison near Summit, Kentucky. He was freed, with time off for good behavior, on December 11, 1951.

Walking the streets of the Kentucky town in which he had been released, waiting for the plane back to New York, Hammett encountered a moonshiner who had also served time. The man was broke, jobless—and Hammett gave him all the money he had, arriving in New York weak from hunger; he'd kept no money to eat with.

Lillian Hellman was there when he got off the plane, and she now saw him as "a thinner man, a sick man." He stumbled coming down the steps, held the rail tightly,

walked slowly over to his old friend. "I guess that was the first time I knew he would now always be sick," she stated.

What irritated her was Hammett's casual, joking attitude toward his five months in prison. ("Dash would always make fun of trouble or pain; that was one way he could handle it.")

Hammett went back to court just a month later to contest a claim by Warner Brothers that he had not had the right to use the character of Sam Spade for his radio show, that the *Falcon* characters belonged to the studio from the moment they purchased all rights. Hammett said no, that he had sold the book to Warners, not the characters. He won, retaining his right to use Spade as he wished.

But, by this time, all of his radio shows were off the air, and the Hollywood moguls did not want an ex-convict writing for them. One more collection, edited by Ellery Queen, *Woman in the Dark* (which contained seven of his Op stories, including the first two Op adventures from 1923, "Arson Plus" and "Slippery Fingers"), appeared in July, 1952. But the follow-up volume, *A Man Named Thin*, promised for quick release, did not appear for a full decade, until the public anti-Hammett mood had been dissipated.

Yet, among critics, Hammett's reputation could not be damaged. In England, a British magazine writer was comparing him with James Joyce, and looked forward with "great excitement" to Hammett's rumored new novel, *There Was a Young Man*. By late May of that year Ben Ray Redman wrote a long essay for *The Saturday Review* in which he attacked Mickey Spillane's brute fiction and lauded Hammett and Chandler as the two modern greats in the detective field. And Clifton Fadiman would later agree: "The school of hard-boiled fiction . . . birthed two masters, [the first] being Dashiell Hammett, whose all-bone style stands out in contrast to Chandler's image-laden raw-colored prose." He spoke of their "class of writing for which we have no name . . . traditionless, close to the violent un-

conscious of the American primitive, remote from any moral universe."

Hammett's long sickness, his exhausting months in prison, had brought him to his knees—but he was not yet completely done as a creative artist. He would produce one final, unfinished work, the novel *Tulip*.

13

THE TOUGH SHELL

Hammett knew that if he were to write the novel he'd been thinking about, planning, making notes for, he'd have to get away from the city, get out into the solitude of the woods and fight the words onto paper. In 1922 he had left his family and "gone to earth" in a San Francisco hotel. Now, thirty years later, he was making another start. He rented a small cottage in Katonah, New York, settling in with his 20-gauge Fox shotgun, his piles of books and phonograph records, his notebooks and papers.

He began to write.

The 18,000-word novel he was to call *Tulip* began to appear, page by slow page. The hero was Hammett himself, an ex-drunk in his fifties, called "Pop," just out of federal prison, who is living in a house in the woods, trying to "get a book started."

Tulip, in Hammett's novel, is a former friend from World War II, a lieutenant colonel Pop had known on Kiska, who comes to the writer and tells him that he wants Pop to do his life story. Pop tells him that he has been trying, for many, many years, to write his own story. Tulip says he is the more interesting of the two, but Pop does not agree. To prove his point, he tells Tulip about some of his adventures during his tuberculosis cure at a hospital near

San Diego, and about some of the early times when he began to write in San Francisco.

Clearly, Hammett was attempting to write his autobiography, through Pop, in novelistic terms.

Throughout the narrative, Hammett keeps returning to Pop's problem, that he cannot write about the things that happened to him beyond his early years. "I've never written a word about any of these things. Why? All I can say is they're not for me. . . . I used to try now and then—but they never came out meaning very much." Later he says, "If you are tired, you ought to rest, I think, and not try to fool yourself and your customers with colored bubbles."

Ironically, Hammett's manuscript ends there (except for a final six-sentence fragment). Hammett had written himself to a standstill, as Pop is at a standstill in the novel. There was nowhere for him to go with the last three-quarters of his book, or so he felt, and the "colored bubbles" ceased to flow.

Tulip is well-written. It involves several other characters who live with Pop at the house; it describes, with precision and knowledge, the woods, lakes, terrain (including a fine, neatly-dialogued duck-hunting sequence). But it is little more than a thinly-disguised cry from Hammett: I can't write! Why can't I write?

Tulip gave Pop no answer; the novel gave its creator no answer. A final impasse had been reached in Hammett's life. His final effort to break down his self-built wall of silence had failed.

At fifty-eight, he was through. There would be no more talk of "making a new start." The last stage of Dashiell Hammett's writing career was over.

By April of 1953 he was back in the headlines—called to testify before Senator Joseph McCarthy's subcommittee investigating charges that pro-Communist books were on the shelves of the Department of State's overseas li-

braries. It worried McCarthy that such books as *The Maltese Falcon* might be circulated out of a U.S. Information Service library. The Senator from Wisconsin was then king of television. His was The Greatest Show on Earth, a TV circus that now had Hammett as one of its star performers.

"Mr. Hammett," intoned the Senator, "if you were spending, as we are, over a hundred million dollars a year on an information program allegedly for the purpose of fighting communism, and if you were in charge of that program to fight communism, would you allow your shelves to bear the work of some seventy-five communist authors, in effect placing our official stamp of approval upon those books?"

Hammett, looking gaunt, with his shock of white hair and sad eyes, shrugged his shoulders, then said, "Well, I think—if I were you, Senator—I would not allow any libraries."

McCarthy chuckled, but the laugh was bitter.

Three hundred copies of Hammett books were removed from the shelves of overseas libraries—prompting Dwight Eisenhower to remark that, in his opinion, the action seemed quite unjustified. "I would not have removed them," he stated. Ike's words eventually took effect, and the Hammett novels were quietly put back into library circulation.

Late in 1956 Hammett was sued by the government for back taxes, and in March of the following year a judgment of $140,000 was filed against him. Yet money was no longer coming in. Although "The Thin Man" was now on television no royalties came to Hammett from the show; he had sold all dramatic rights.

Now his summers were spent at Vineyard Haven, Massachusetts, on the island of Martha's Vineyard, in a high frame house with yellow shingles and climbing roses, with a view of the passing Nantucket ferries available from the windows of its box-like rooms. Built like a century-old

Yankee farmhouse, it contained, in the far east wing, a tower formed by the hollow shell of an ancient Cape Cod windmill. Hammett lived in the tower.

"He escaped there when company arrived," says a friend. "He had become a recluse, and near the end of his life he talked to almost nobody. His clear-eyed, lean, aristocratic face would deliver a beatific smile to any visitor who might catch him off-guard in the main part of the house, but when the visitor turned to speak to him again he'd have vanished into his tower retreat. . . . He was at the end of his strength, often too weak to take his meals at the table."

In November of 1960 Hammett was examined by a doctor. Cancer of the lungs. Not operable.

"He did not wish to die and I like to think he didn't know he was dying," says Lillian Hellman.

Hammett suffered privately, asked for little. He ate only a small portion of the food set before him, read sparingly.

By New Year's Eve, however, his endurance was at an end. Hammett had told Lillian to go out, see some friends, enjoy herself—and she did, reluctantly leaving him under the care of a practical nurse. He told her that he would have a Happy New Year in bed.

She came home shortly after midnight to find that the nurse had been trying to reach her. His condition was critical. Hammett was taken to Lenox Hill Hospital, but he did not improve. He went into coma.

Two days later, on January 10, 1961, he died—just four and a half months from his sixty-seventh birthday.

Hammett had asked to be buried at Arlington Cemetery—and at his funeral Lillian Hellman delivered the memorial address, declaring that "he would not have wanted many words today. He was a man who respected words in books, but suspected words in life. He believed that they sometimes took the place of thought, and almost

always took the place of action, and he deeply believed in both . . . he was a man of simple honor and great bravery . . . most of his life was open and adventurous. He grew and learned and acted on what he learned . . . he believed in the salvation of intelligence, and he tried to live it out . . . and never, in all the years, did he play anybody's game but his own. He never lied, he never faked, he never stooped . . . he seemed to me a great man."

Hammett left a quarter of his estate (less than $10,000) to Lillian Hellman, the remainder to his two daughters in California, Mrs. Josephine Marshall of Camarillo and Mrs. Mary Miller of Los Angeles.

In its obituary, the New York *Times* said of him: "His prose was clean and entirely unique. His characters were as sharply and economically defined as any in American fiction. His stories were as consistent as mathematics and as intricate as psychology . . . the Latin scholar responded to the classic precision of his language and the comic strip reader to the excitement of his plots."

In *The National Review*, Donald Phelps praised Hammett for "dictating a new form for the detective novel. His detective is a man . . . who may not re-order the world, but who tries rather to maintain in that world his own track of integrity, professional fidelity and . . . his own sort of gallantry."

And Frederick Gardner declared, in *The Nation*: "He did for American slang—the argot of hobos, cowboys, seamen, boxers, longshoremen, miners, cops, and robbers—what Mark Twain had previously done for the American vernacular: used it on the level of art."

Hammett had written his own epitaph some three decades earlier, when his Op describes a certain character who would not back down, even as he lay dying: "He meant to die as he had lived, inside the same tough shell."

Samuel Dashiell Hammett, the man whose fiction changed the course of popular literature, did just that.

A DASHIELL HAMMETT CHECK-LIST

NO FULL Hammett check-list has heretofore been assembled. The two previous listings—by Ellery Queen (Frederic Dannay and Manfred B. Lee) in *A Man Named Thin,* and by Roger E. Stoddard in London's *The Book Collector*—dealt exclusively with Hammett's books. The present check-list covers the author's work in a variety of fields, but does not include magazine reprints or foreign book reprints.

It is arranged in the following sections:

Books
Magazine Fiction
Articles
Introductions
Poetry
Reviews
Letters
Newspaper Work
Radio Work
Motion Pictures
Anthology Appearances

BOOKS

RED HARVEST. Alfred A. Knopf, Inc.: 1929
This novel originally appeared as four separate novelets in *Black Mask* from November, 1927 through February, 1928.

THE DAIN CURSE. Alfred A. Knopf, Inc.: 1929
This novel originally appeared as four separate novelets in *Black Mask* from November, 1928 through February, 1929.

THE MALTESE FALCON. Alfred A. Knopf, Inc.: 1930
This novel originally appeared as a five-part serial in *Black Mask* from September, 1929 through January, 1930. A Modern Library edition, with a special Hammett introduction, was published in 1934.

THE GLASS KEY. Alfred A. Knopf, Inc.: 1931
This novel originally appeared as four separate novelets in *Black Mask* from March, 1930 through June, 1930.

CREEPS BY NIGHT. The John Day Company: 1931
This anthology, edited and with an introduction by Hammett, contains 20 tales of terror and the supernatural. The authors include William Faulkner, John Collier, André Maurois, Conrad Aiken, et al. (In England, this collection was published as *Modern Tales of Horror* in hard covers and, condensed, as *The Red Brain* in paperback.)

THE THIN MAN. Alfred A. Knopf, Inc.: 1934
This novel, slightly condensed, appeared in *Redbook*, December, 1933.

SECRET AGENT X-9. (Book 1) David McKay Company: 1934
A paperbound compilation of the King Features comic strip, written by Hammett and drawn by Alex Raymond. (Contains the first portion of X-9's initial adventure.)

SECRET AGENT X-9. (Book 2) David McKay Company: 1934
A continuation of the Hammett/Raymond strip, and a completion of the first adventure.

BLOOD MONEY. World Publishing Company: 1943
A first hard-cover printing of the story which had originally been printed, as two novelets, in *Black Mask* for February and May, 1927. Appeared four months earlier in paperback from Lawrence E. Spivak as *$106,000 Blood Money*. (A Spivak reissue, condensed, bore the title *The Big Knock-Over* in 1948.)

THE BATTLE OF THE ALEUTIANS. Produced by the Intelligence Section, Field Force Headquarters, Adak, Alaska: 1944
This paperbound pamphlet, sub-titled *A Graphic History, 1942–1943*, was co-written by Hammett (then Cpl. Hammett) and Cpl. Robert Colodny. It forms an illustrated campaign history of the war in the Aleutians.

THE ADVENTURES OF SAM SPADE AND OTHER STORIES. World Publishing Company: 1945
Introduction by Ellery Queen.
A collection containing:
"Too Many Have Lived"
"They Can Only Hang You Once"
"A Man Called Spade"
"The Assistant Murderer"
"Night Shade"
"The Judge Laughed Last"
"His Brother's Keeper"

Several variant paperback editions appeared, the first preceding the hard-cover World edition, from Lawrence E. Spivak in 1944. (This collection was reissued, with partial contents, as *A Man Called Spade and Other Stories* from Dell in 1945. Later issued, unabridged, as *They Can Only Hang You Once and Other Stories* from Spivak in 1949.)

THE CONTINENTAL OP. Lawrence E. Spivak: 1945
Introduction by Ellery Queen.
A paperback collection containing:
"Fly Paper"
"Death on Pine Street"
"Zigzags of Treachery"
"The Farewell Murder"
Never released in hard-cover format.

THE RETURN OF THE CONTINENTAL OP. Lawrence E. Spivak: 1945
Introduction by Ellery Queen.
A paperback collection containing:
"The Whosis Kid"
"The Gutting of Couffignal"
"Death and Company"
"One Hour"
"The Tenth Clue"
Never released in hard-cover format.

HAMMETT HOMICIDES. Lawrence E. Spivak: 1946
Introduction and prefaces by Ellery Queen.
A paperback collection containing:
"The House in Turk Street"
"The Girl With the Silver Eyes"
"Night Shots"
"The Main Death"
"Two Sharp Knives"
"Ruffian's Wife"
Never released in hard-cover format.

DEAD YELLOW WOMEN. Lawrence E. Spivak: 1947
Introduction and notes by Ellery Queen.
A paperback collection containing:
"Dead Yellow Women"

"The Golden Horseshoe"
"House Dick"
"Who Killed Bob Teal?"
"The Green Elephant"
"The Hairy One"
Never released in hard-cover format.

NIGHTMARE TOWN. Lawrence E. Spivak: 1948
Introduction by Ellery Queen.
A paperback collection containing:
"Nightmare Town"
"The Scorched Face"
"Albert Pastor at Home"
"Corkscrew"
Never released in hard-cover format.

THE CREEPING SIAMESE. Lawrence E. Spivak: 1950
Introduction by Ellery Queen.
A paperback collection containing:
"The Creeping Siamese"
"The Man Who Killed Dan Odams"
"The Nails in Mr. Cayterer"
"The Joke on Eloise Morey"
"Tom, Dick or Harry"
"This King Business"
Never released in hard-cover format.

WOMAN IN THE DARK. Lawrence E. Spivak: 1952
Introduction and with a story preface by Ellery Queen.
A paperback collection containing:
"Arson Plus"
"Slippery Fingers"
"The Black Hat That Wasn't There"
"Woman in the Dark"
"Afraid of a Gun"
"Holiday"
"The Man Who Stood in the Way"
Never released in hard-cover format.

A MAN NAMED THIN. Joseph W. Ferman: 1962
Introduction and prefaces by Ellery Queen, with a check-list of Hammett books.

A paperback collection containing:
"A Man Named Thin"
"Wages of Crime"
"The Gatewood Caper"
"The Barber and His Wife"
"Itchy the Debonair"
"The Second-Story Angel"
"In the Morgue"
"When Luck's Running Good"
Never released in hard-cover format.

THE BIG KNOCKOVER. Random House, Inc.: 1966
Introduction by Lillian Hellman.
A hard-cover collection containing:
"The Gutting of Couffignal"
"Fly Paper"
"The Scorched Face"
"This King Business"
"The Gatewood Caper"
"Dead Yellow Women"
"Corkscrew"
"Tulip"
"The Big Knockover"
"$106,000 Blood Money"
All of these stories (with the exception of "Tulip") appeared in the various Hammett paperback collections supervised by Ellery Queen. "Tulip" appears for the first time in print—an unfinished Hammett novel.

The full-text omnibus volume containing Hammett's five major novels (*Red Harvest, The Dain Curse, The Máltese Falcon, The Glass Key* and *The Thin Man*) with a brief note on Hammett by Lillian Hellman was published by Knopf in 1965 as *The Novels of Dashiell Hammett,* and is highly recommended.

Regarding Hammett reprint editions: it is distressingly easy to become confused over Hammett's paperback reprints. When Dell released the Hellman-edited collection, *The Big Knockover,* in paperback format, they split the contents into two editions, *The Big Knockover* and *The Continental Op.* The latter should not be confused with the earlier volume of

the same title, edited by Ellery Queen, and also reprinted by Dell some years earlier. (Several other Hammett titles edited by Queen were reprinted by Dell. These were of special interest due to their back-cover maps of San Francisco, pinpointing the areas involved in Hammett's stories. Curiously, the Dell edition of *Blood Money* added chapter titles to the book.)

Among foreign-language reprints, perhaps the most unusual item is the 238-page Italian edition (from Fratelli Spada in 1965) of *Secret Agent X-9,* which, as *Agente Segreto X9* is bylined "di Alex Raymond." Absolutely no credit is given to Hammett anywhere in this collection of his first three X-9 adventures (which date from January 1934 into March of 1935).

The range of Hammett reprint book editions is exemplified by *The Maltese Falcon,* in comic-book format, issued by King Features in 1946, illustrated by Rodlow Willard.

Of British editions, *The Dashiell Hammett Omnibus* (Cassell: 1950) is valuable in that it not only reprints the five major Hammett novels, but contains four Continental Op short stories in hard-cover for the first time in a Hammett collection: "Dead Yellow Women," "The Golden Horseshoe," "House Dick," and "Who Killed Bob Teal?" (Lillian Hellman picked up the first of these for her *Big Knockover* collection in 1966, but the others remain uncollected in hard-cover in the States.)

MAGAZINE FICTION

SINCE THERE WERE NO RECORDS kept of Hammett's early magazine work it is possible that several of his stories remain buried in obscure, non-indexed publications of the Twenties. Of the following 74 magazine titles, 38 have been printed in hard-cover format in the U.S. (30 as Hammett novels or as part of his hard-cover collections, *The Adventures of Sam Spade* and *The Big Knockover,* the final eight in non-Hammett hard-cover anthologies). Of the remaining titles, 31 are preserved only in paperback format, and five have never been collected. Since a full anthology listing is included elsewhere in this check-list, no attempt has been made here to indicate a title's inclusion in anthology form unless—as with the eight special titles—the story's only hard-cover appearance was in an anthology. Continental Op stories are marked with an asterisk.

1922

"The Barber and His Wife." (by "Peter Collinson") *Brief Stories,* December

Included in Hammett collection: *A Man Named Thin.*

"The Road Home." (by "Peter Collinson") *Black Mask,* December

Hammett's first contribution to this magazine. Not collected.

1923

"The Sardonic Star of Tom Doody." (by "Peter Collinson") *Brief Stories,* February

Included (under title "Wages of Crime") in Hammett collection: *A Man Named Thin.*

"The Joke on Eloise Morey." *Brief Stories,* June
Included in Hammett collection: *The Creeping Siamese.*

"The Vicious Circle." (by "Peter Collinson") *Black Mask,* June 15
Included (under title "The Man Who Stood in the Way") in Hammett collection: *Woman in the Dark.*

"Holiday." *Pearson's Magazine,* July
Included in Hammett collection: *Woman in the Dark.*

"The Crusader." (by "Mary Jane Hammett") *Smart Set,* August
Not collected.

"Arson Plus."* (by "Peter Collinson") *Black Mask,* October 1
Included in Hammett collection: *Woman in the Dark.* The first Continental Op story.

"Slippery Fingers."* (by "Peter Collinson") *Black Mask,* October 15
Included in Hammett collection: *Woman in the Dark.* This issue of *BM* was the only one to carry both a "Collinson" and a Hammett story.

"Crooked Souls."* *Black Mask,* October 15
Included (under title "The Gatewood Caper") in Hammett collections: *A Man Named Thin* and *The Big Knockover.* The first use of Hammett's name on a *BM* story.

"The Dimple." *Saucy Stories,* October 15
Included (under title "In the Morgue") in Hammett collection: *A Man Named Thin.*

"The Green Elephant." *Smart Set,* October
Included in Hammett collection: *Dead Yellow Women.* Anthologized in hard-cover: *The Smart Set Anthology.*

"It."* *Black Mask,* November 1
Included (under title "The Black Hat That Wasn't There") in Hammett collection: *Woman in the Dark.*

"The Second-Story Angel." *Black Mask,* November 15
Included in Hammett collection: *A Man Named Thin.*

"Bodies Piled Up."* *Black Mask,* December 1
Included (under title "House Dick") in Hammett collection: *Dead Yellow Women.*

"Laughing Masks." Magazine origin unknown.
Included (under title "When Luck's Running Good") in Hammett collection: *A Man Named Thin.*

1924

"The Tenth Clew."* *Black Mask,* January 1
Included (under title "The Tenth Clue") in Hammett collection: *The Return of the Continental Op.* Anthologized in hard-cover: *Fourth Mystery Companion.*

"The Man Who Killed Dan Odams." *Black Mask,* January 15
Included in Hammett collection: *The Creeping Siamese.*

"Itchy." *Brief Stories,* January
Included (under title "Itchy the Debonair") in Hammett collection: *A Man Named Thin.*

"Esther Entertains." *Brief Stories,* February
Not collected.

"Night Shots."* *Black Mask,* February 1
Included in Hammett collection: *Hammett Homicides.*

"The New Racket." *Black Mask,* February 15
Included (under title "The Judge Laughed Last") in Hammett collection: *The Adventures of Sam Spade.*

"Afraid of a Gun." *Black Mask,* March 1
Included in Hammett collection: *Woman in the Dark.*

"Zigzags of Treachery."* *Black Mask,* March 1
Included in Hammett collection: *The Continental Op.* In same issue with "Afraid of a Gun."

"One Hour."* *Black Mask,* April 1.
Included in Hammett collection: *The Return of the Continental Op.*

"The House in Turk Street."* *Black Mask,* April 15
Included in Hammett collection: *Hammett Homicides.*

"The Girl With the Silver Eyes."* *Black Mask,* June
Included in Hammett collection: *Hammett Homicides.* A sequel to "The House in Turk Street."

"Women, Politics and Murder."* *Black Mask,* September
Included (under title "Death on Pine Street") in Hammett collection: *The Continental Op.*

"The Golden Horseshoe."* *Black Mask,* November
Included in Hammett collection: *Dead Yellow Women.*

"Who Killed Bob Teal?"* *True Detective,* November
Included in Hammett collection: *Dead Yellow Women.*

"Nightmare Town." *Argosy All-Story,* December 27
Included in Hammett collection: *Nightmare Town.*

1925

"Mike, Alec or Rufus."* *Black Mask,* January
Included (under title "Tom, Dick or Harry") in Hammett collection: *The Creeping Siamese.* Anthologized in hardcover: *Twentieth Century Detective Stories*

"Ber-Bulu." *Sunset Magazine,* March
Included (under title "The Hairy One") in Hammett collection: *Dead Yellow Women.*

"The Whosis Kid."* *Black Mask,* March
Included in Hammett collection: *The Return of the Continental Op.*

"The Scorched Face."* *Black Mask,* May
Included in Hammett collections: *Nightmare Town* and *The Big Knockover.*

"Corkscrew."* *Black Mask,* September
Included in Hammett collections: *Nightmare Town* and *The Big Knockover.*

"Ruffian's Wife." *Sunset Magazine,* October
Included in Hammett collection: *Hammett Homicides.* Anthologized in hard-cover: *Rogue's Gallery.*

"Dead Yellow Women."* *Black Mask,* November
Included in Hammett collections: *Dead Yellow Women* and *The Big Knockover.*

"The Gutting of Couffignal."* *Black Mask,* December
Included in Hammett collections: *The Return of the Continental Op* and *The Big Knockover.*

1926

"The Nails in Mr. Cayterer." *Black Mask,* January
Included in Hammett collection: *The Creeping Siamese.* The first of his two "Robin Thin" stories.

"The Assistant Murderer." *Black Mask,* February
Included in Hammett collection: *The Adventures of Sam Spade.*

"Creeping Siamese."* *Black Mask,* March
Included in Hammett collection: *The Creeping Siamese.*

1927

"The Big Knockover."* *Black Mask,* February
Included as first half of his novel, *Blood Money,* and in Hammett collection: *The Big Knockover.*

"$106,000 Blood Money."* *Black Mask,* May
Included as second half of his novel, *Blood Money,* and in Hammett collection: *The Big Knockover.*

"The Main Death."* *Black Mask,* June
Included in Hammett collection: *Hammett Homicides.*

"The Cleansing of Poisonville."* *Black Mask,* November
Revised as part 1 of his novel, *Red Harvest.*

"Crime Wanted—Male or Female."* *Black Mask*, December
Revised as part 2 of his novel, *Red Harvest.*

1928

"This King Business."* *Mystery Stories*, January
Included in Hammett collections: *The Creeping Siamese* and *The Big Knockover.*

"Dynamite."* *Black Mask*, January
Revised as part 3 of his novel, *Red Harvest.*

"The 19th Murder."* *Black Mask*, February
Revised as part 4 of his novel, *Red Harvest.*

"Black Lives."* *Black Mask*, November
Revised as part 1 of his novel, *The Dain Curse.*

"The Hollow Temple."* *Black Mask*, December
Revised as part 2 of his novel, *The Dain Curse.*

1929

"Black Honeymoon."* *Black Mask*, January
Revised as part 3 of his novel, *The Dain Curse.*

"Black Riddle."* *Black Mask*, February
Revised as part 4 of his novel, *The Dain Curse.*

"Fly Paper."* *Black Mask*, August
Included in Hammett collections: *The Continental Op* and *The Big Knockover.*

"The Diamond Wager." (by "Samuel Dashiell") *Detective Fiction Weekly*, October 19
Not collected.

"The Maltese Falcon." *Black Mask* (a 5-part serial), September, October, November, December. Concluded in January of 1930.
Revised as a published novel.

1930

"The Farewell Murder."* *Black Mask*, February
Included in Hammett collection: *The Continental Op.*

Anthologized in hard-cover: *Best American Mystery Stories of the Year.*

"The Glass Key." *Black Mask,* March
Revised as part 1 of his novel of the same title.

"The Cyclone Shot." *Black Mask,* April
Revised as part 2 of his novel, *The Glass Key.*

"Dagger Point." *Black Mask,* May
Revised as part 3 of his novel, *The Glass Key.*

"The Shattered Key." *Black Mask,* June
Revised as part 4 of his novel, *The Glass Key.*

"Death and Company."* *Black Mask,* November
Included in Hammett collection: *The Return of the Continental Op.* Hammett's last *Black Mask* story and the final one in the Op series. Anthologized in hard-cover: *Best American Mystery Stories of the Year.*

1932

"A Man Called Spade." *American Magazine,* July
Included in Hammett collection: *The Adventures of Sam Spade.*

"Too Many Have Lived." *American Magazine,* October
Included in Hammett collection: *The Adventures of Sam Spade.* The second Spade short story.

"They Can Only Hang You Once." *Collier's,* November 19
Included in Hammett collection: *The Adventures of Sam Spade.* The third and final Spade short story.

1933

"Woman in the Dark." *Liberty* (a 3-part serial), April 8, April 15, and April 22
Included in Hammett collection: *Woman in the Dark.*

"Albert Pastor at Home." *Esquire,* Autumn
Included in Hammett collection: *Nightmare Town.*

"Night Shade." *Mystery League,* October
Included in Hammett collection: *The Adventures of Sam Spade.*

"The Thin Man." *Redbook,* December
A slightly-condensed version of the published novel.

1934

"Two Sharp Knives." *Collier's,* January 13
Included in Hammett collection: *Hammett Homicides.*
Anthologized in hard-cover: *Stories for Men.*

"His Brother's Keeper." *Collier's,* February 17
Included in Hammett collection: *The Adventures of Sam Spade.*

"This Little Pig." *Collier's,* March 24
Not collected.

1961

"A Man Named Thin." *Ellery Queen's Mystery Magazine,* March
Included in Hammett collection: *A Man Named Thin.* The second "Robin Thin" story. Anthologized in hard-cover: *Ellery Queen's 16th Mystery Annual.*

ARTICLES

"The Master Mind." *Smart Set*, January, 1923

"From the Memoirs of a Private Detective." *Smart Set*, March, 1923

"In Defense of the Sex Story." *Writer's Digest*, June, 1924

"Finger-Prints." *Black Mask*, June, 1925

"Tempo in the Novel." *Fighting Words*, edited by Donald Ogden Stewart. Harcourt, Brace: 1940

A speech-into-article, from a chapter on the craft of the novel.

INTRODUCTIONS

to his edited collection: *Creeps by Night*. The John Day Company: 1931

to a special edition of *The Maltese Falcon*. Modern Library: 1934

to *The Communist Trial* by George Marion. Fairplay: 1950

POETRY

"Curse in the Old Manner." *Bookman*, September, 1927

Several of Hammett's stories contain poetry, and two of them deal with "Robin Thin," a poet-detective. Also, in her introduction to *The Big Knockover*, Lillian Hellman states that Hammett contributed "squibs and . . . poems to Mencken's *Smart Set*."

REVIEWS

APPARENTLY HAMMETT HAD SEVERAL reviews published early in his career. In the autobiographical novel, *Tulip*, he reprints a review of Edward Waite's *The Brotherhood of the Rosy Cross* (pages 249–251 in his collection, *The Big Knockover*) quoting the source as "a weekly that had gone out of existence in the depression days of the early 30s." The review originally appeared during 1924, the year of the book's publication.

Hammett reviewed the following 11 books for *The Saturday Review of Literature* between January 15, 1927 and October 26, 1929:

The Benson Murder Case by S.S. Van Dine. January 15, 1927
The Massingham Butterfly by J.S. Fletcher. January 15, 1927
The House of Sin by Allen Upward. May 21, 1927
The Lost Adventurer by Walter Gilkyson. June 11, 1927
The Man Who Killed Fortescue by John Stephen Strange. October 13, 1928
The Unpleasantness at the Bellona Club by Dorothy L. Sayers. October 27, 1928
The Female of the Species by H. C. McNeile. January 5, 1929
Murder Mansion by Herman Landon. January 12, 1929
Lord Peter Views the Body by Dorothy L. Sayers. May 4, 1929
The Needle's Kiss by Austin J. Small. September 7, 1929
Mystery at Spanish Hacienda by Jackson Gregory. October 26, 1929

Hammett reviewed the following 62 books for the New York *Evening Post* between April 5 and October 11, 1930:

The Door by Mary Roberts Rinehart. April 5

Following Footsteps by Joseph J. Fargeon. April 12
The Noose by Philip MacDonald. April 12
Black Door by Virgil Markham. April 12
The Blue Room by Ernest Souza. April 12
The Wychford Poisoning Case by Anthony Berkeley. April 26
Murder in the State Department by "Diplomat." April 26
Why Murder the Judge? by Claude S. Hammock. April 26
Through the Eyes of the Judge by Bruce Graeme. April 26
Marked Cancelled by Natalie Sumner Lincoln. April 26
Death Traps by Kay Strahan. April 26
Yorkshire Moorland Murder by J.S. Fletcher. May 10
The Case of the Marsden Rubies by Leonard R. Gribble. May 10
Ladies' Man by Rupert Hughes. May 10
Man of a Hundred Faces by Gaston Leroux. May 10
The Death of Cosmo Revere by Christopher Bush. May 24
The Man Who was There by N. A. Temple-Ellis. May 24
What Happened to Forester? by E. Phillips Oppenheim. May 24
The Scarab Murder Case by S.S. Van Dine. May 24
Manhattan Night by William A. Wolff. May 24
The Valley of Creeping Men by Rayburn Crawley. June 7
The Voice in the Closet by Herman Landon. June 7
The Other Bullet by Nancy Mavitt. June 7
The Thirty-First Bullfinch by Helen Reilly. June 7
The Case of Robert Robertson by S.C. Svendson Elvestad. June 21
The Owner Lies Dead by Tyline Perry. June 21
The Rhododendron Man by John A. Tyson. June 21
The Square Mark by Grace White and Hilda L. Deakin. June 21
The Hand of Power by Edgar Wallace. July 5
The Yellow Crystal by Anthony Wynne. July 5
The Murder of Cecily Thane by Harriette Ashbrook. July 19
Murder on the Bridge by Alister McAllister. July 19
Green Ice by Raoul Whitfield. July 19
The Actress by Julian Swift. August 23
The Redman Cave Murder by Elsa Barker. August 23
Four Armourers by Francis Beeding. August 23
The Opium Murders by Peter Baron. August 23
The Silver King Mystery by Ian B. Greig. August 23
Is No One Innocent? by Milton H. Gropper and Edna Sherry, August 23

Scalps by Murray Leinster. August 23
Trail of Scotland Yard by Stuart Martin. August 23
The Two Ticket Puzzle by J. J. Connington. August 23
The Marston Murder Case by William Averill Stowell. August 23
The Secret of the Bungalow by Robert J. Casey. September 6
Man in the Red Hat by Richard Keverne. September 6
Back Bay Murders by Roger Scarlett. September 6
Did She Fall? by Thorne Smith. September 6
The Strangler Fig by John Stephen Strange. September 6
Alibi by Frederic F. Van de Water. September 6
Backstage Mystery by Octavus Roy Cohen. September 20
The South Foreland Murder by J. S. Fletcher. September 20
The Splendid Crime by Alan Dare. September 20
The Saranoff Murder by Mark Luther and Lillian C. Ford. September 20
Private Life by Paul Selver. September 20
The Blue Door by Vincent Starrett. September 20
The Case of Anne Bickerton by S. Fowler Wright. September 20
The Garston Murder Case by H. C. Bailey. October 11
Charlie Chan Carries On by Earl Derr Biggers. October 11
I Met Murder by Selwyn Jepson. October 11
Swan Island Murders by Victoria Lincoln. October 11
The Murderer Returns by Edwin Torgerson. October 11
Ghosts' High Noon by Carolyn Wells. October 11

Excerpts from many of these reviews may be found, under the individual author's name, in *Book Review Digest* for 1930, carried at most libraries. This listing was prepared with the generous help of William J. Clark.

LETTERS

Many of the *Black Mask* letters from Hammett appeared in "Our Readers Private Corner" section at the back of the magazine, sometimes under the heading "Inside Dope From Authors."

From the Author of "The Vicious Circle." *Black Mask,* June 15, 1923

Although this story was bylined "Peter Collinson," the letter from the author was signed "S.D. Hammett."

From the Author of "Arson Plus." *Black Mask,* October 1, 1923

From the Author of "Slippery Fingers." *Black Mask,* October 15, 1923

From the Author of "The Tenth Clew." *Black Mask,* January 1, 1924

From the Author of "Afraid of a Gun." *Black Mask,* March 1, 1924

From the Author of "Zigzags of Treachery." *Black Mask,* March 1, 1924

"Let's Wait." *Black Mask,* March 15, 1924

A letter from Hammett regarding an editorial story idea.

"The Girl With the Silver Eyes." *Black Mask,* June, 1924

"Our Own Short Story Course." *Black Mask,* August, 1924
A discussion of two rejected stories with a letter of comment from Hammett.

"Three Favorites." *Black Mask,* November, 1924
A trio of autobiographical letters from Francis James, Carroll John Daly, and Hammett, with photographs.

"Behind the Mask." *Black Mask,* June, 1930.

A letter from Hammett is quoted in Joseph T. Shaw's introduction to *The Hard-Boiled Omnibus.* Simon and Schuster, Inc.: 1946

A letter from Hammett (dated January 14, 1942) is included in *The Boys in the Black Mask.* U.C.L.A.: 1961

NEWSPAPER WORK

Aside from book reviews, Hammett's main contribution to newspapers was his daily strip, "Secret Agent X-9," which he created and wrote for King Features Syndicate, beginning in 1934 and extending into 1939. (The strip was continued beyond this date by other writers.)

Hammett also edited and published a daily service newspaper during World War II, while stationed in Alaska.

RADIO WORK

HAMMETT WAS DIRECTLY connected with three very successful radio series which were broadcast in the early 1940s to early 1950s:

"The Thin Man." Starred Les Damon as "Nick Charles." (The role was also handled by Les Tremayne, Joseph Curtin and David Gothard.) Claudia Morgan played "Nora." Himan Brown was producer-director. Milton Lewis, Eugene Wang and Robert Newman wrote the scripts. Hammett worked on this series in the early Forties.

"The Adventures of Sam Spade." Starred Howard Duff in the title role. (Later handled by Steve Dunne.) Lurene Tuttle played "Effie." William Spier directed, beginning in July of 1946. Gil Doud and Bob Tallman wrote most of the scripts. Hammett worked on this series from its inception, but there is no record of the exact number of scripts he contributed.

"The Fat Man." Starred J. Scott Smart as "Brad Runyon." Ed Begley played "Sgt. O'Hara." Clark Andrews and Charles Powers directed. Robert Sloane was the chief writer. Hammett created this series especially for radio, and worked on several of the early episodes.

The Lux Radio Theater presented three Hammett shows between 1936 and early 1943:

"The Thin Man." Broadcast on June 8, 1936, based on the MGM film script and starring William Powell and Myrna Loy in their original roles. W.S. Van Dyke was producer-director.

"After the Thin Man." Broadcast on June 17, 1940, based on the MGM film script and again starring Powell and Loy. Cecil B. DeMille produced.

"The Maltese Falcon." Broadcast on February 8, 1943, based on the Warner Brothers film script and starring Edward G. Robinson as "Spade," Gail Patrick as "Brigid" and Laird Cregar as "Gutman." Supporting roles included Bea Benederet as "Effie," Eddie Marr as "Wilmer" and Charlie Lung as "Cairo." Cecil B. DeMille produced.

In 1939, Orson Welles presented "The Glass Key" on radio's Campbell Playhouse. Welles did the adaptation of Hammett's novel for this production.

In 1942, *Click* ran a "photo-story" under the Hammett byline, "The Thin Man and the Flack," which was adapted from one of his radio scripts.

MOTION PICTURES

HAMMETT WENT TO HOLLYWOOD in 1930 to write for the screen. He left Hollywood in 1942. During this period he was credited with one screenplay, and contributed original screen stories on at least six credited productions. Much of his work, in "polish" form, went uncredited.

ROADHOUSE NIGHTS. Paramount: 1930. Starring: Helen Morgan, Charles Ruggles, Fred Kohler, Jimmy Durante.
Directed by Hobart Henley.
Screenplay by Garrett Fort, from a story by Ben Hecht, "The River Inn."
This film is "based" on the novel, *Red Harvest,* but retains nothing of the plot. Hammett received no official screen credit.

CITY STREETS. Paramount: 1931. Starring: Gary Cooper, Sylvia Sidney, Paul Lukas, William Boyd.
Directed by Rouben Mamoulian and produced by E. Lloyd Sheldon.
Screenplay by Oliver H.P. Garrett, from the adaptation by Max Marcin.
From an original screen story by Hammett, "After School."

THE MALTESE FALCON. Warner Brothers: 1931. Starring: Ricardo Cortez, Bebe Daniels, Dudley Digges, Una Merkel.

Directed by Roy Del Ruth.
Screenplay by Maude Fulton, Lucien Hubbard and Brown Holmes.
From Hammett's novel—the first of three film versions.

THE THIN MAN. Metro-Goldwyn-Mayer: 1934. Starring: William Powell, Myrna Loy, Maureen O'Sullivan, Nat Pendleton.
Directed by W.S. Van Dyke and produced by Hunt Stromberg.
Screenplay by Albert Hackett and Frances Goodrich.
From Hammett's novel. (He was on the set during production, and may have contributed polish dialogue to the final version.)

WOMAN IN THE DARK. RKO Radio: 1934. Starring: Fay Wray, Ralph Bellamy, Melvyn Douglas, Roscoe Ates.
Directed by Phil Rosen and produced by Burt Kelly for Select Productions.
Screenplay by Sada Cowan, with additional dialogue by Charles Williams and Marcy Klauber.
From the *Liberty* serial-story by Hammett.

MISTER DYNAMITE. Universal: 1935. Starring: Edmund Lowe, Jean Dixon, Esther Ralston, Victor Varconi.
Directed by Alan Crosland and produced by E. M. Asher.
Screenplay by Doris Malloy and Harry Clork.
From Hammett's original screen story, "On the Make." (Lowe plays a Spade-like private detective named "Dynamite" and the action is set in San Francisco.)

THE GLASS KEY. Paramount: 1935. Starring: George Raft, Edward Arnold, Claire Dodd, Ray Milland.
Directed by Frank Tuttle and produced by E. Lloyd Sheldon.
Screenplay by Kathryn Scola and Kubec Glasmon, with additional dialogue by Harry Ruskin.
From Hammett's novel—the first of two film versions.

SATAN MET A LADY. Warner Brothers: 1936. Starring: Bette Davis, Warren William, Alison Skipworth, Arthur Treacher.

Directed by William Dieterle and produced by Henry Blanke.

Screenplay by Brown Holmes.

The second version of "The Maltese Falcon." A trade paper of this period reported that another original Hammett story, "Money Man," also formed part of the plot basis.

AFTER THE THIN MAN. Metro-Goldwyn-Mayer: 1936. Starring: William Powell, Myrna Loy, James Stewart, Elissa Landi.

Directed by W.S. Van Dyke and produced by Hunt Stromberg.

Screenplay by Frances Goodrich and Albert Hackett.

From an original screen story by Hammett. (He based at least one incident in this film on his original unpublished manuscript version of "The Thin Man," written in 1930.)

ANOTHER THIN MAN. Metro-Goldwyn-Mayer: 1939. Starring: William Powell, Myrna Loy, Virginia Grey, Otto Kruger.

Directed by W.S. Van Dyke and produced by Hunt Stromberg.

Screenplay by Frances Goodrich and Albert Hackett, with additional (uncredited) screen material from Anita Loos.

From an original screen story by Hammett.

THE MALTESE FALCON. Warner Brothers: 1941. Starring: Humphrey Bogart, Mary Astor, Peter Lorre, Sydney Greenstreet.

Directed by John Huston and produced by Henry Blanke.

Screenplay by John Huston.

The final, famous version of the Hammett novel. Huston's screenplay was almost a literal transcription of the book, retaining most of Hammett's dialogue.

SHADOW OF THE THIN MAN. Metro-Goldwyn-Mayer: 1941. Starring: William Powell, Myrna Loy, Barry Nelson, Donna Reed.

Directed by W.S. Van Dyke and produced by Hunt Stromberg.

Screenplay by Irving Brecher and Harry Kurnitz, from an original story by Harry Kurnitz.

Based on the Hammett characters.

THE GLASS KEY. Paramount: 1942. Starring: Alan Ladd, Veronica Lake, Brian Donlevy, William Bendix.

Directed by Stuart Heisler and produced by Fred Kohlmar.

Screenplay by Jonathan Latimer.

The second screen version of the Hammett novel.

WATCH ON THE RHINE. Warner Brothers: 1943. Starring: Bette Davis, Paul Lukas, Geraldine Fitzgerald, Lucile Watson.

Directed by Herman Shumlin and produced by Hal B. Wallis.

Screenplay by Dashiell Hammett, based on the play by Lillian Hellman—with additional scenes and dialogue by Lillian Hellman.

Hammett's only screenplay credit, a very faithful adaptation of the stage play.

THE THIN MAN GOES HOME. Metro-Goldwyn-Mayer: 1944. Starring: William Powell, Myrna Loy, Lucile Watson, Gloria DeHaven.

Directed by Richard Thorpe and produced by Everett Riskin.

Screenplay by Robert Riskin and Dwight Taylor, from a treatment by Harry Kurnitz, based on an original story by Riskin and Kurnitz.

Based on the Hammett characters.

SONG OF THE THIN MAN. Metro-Goldwyn-Mayer: 1947. Starring: William Powell, Myrna Loy, Keenan Wynn, Dean Stockwell.

Directed by Edward Buzzell and produced by Nat Perrin.

Screenplay by Steve Fisher and Nat Perrin, with additional dialogue by James O'Hanlon and Harry Crane, from an original story by Stanley Roberts.

Based on the Hammett characters.

THE FAT MAN. Universal-International: 1951. Starring J.

Scott Smart, Julie London, Rock Hudson, Jayne Meadows.

Directed by William Castle and produced by Aubrey Schenck.

Screenplay by Harry Essex and Leonard Lee, from an original story by Leonard Lee.

Based on the Hammett radio character.

This listing was prepared with the generous help of Clifford McCarty.

ANTHOLOGY APPEARANCES

The selections chosen for this anthology listing reflect the total range of Hammett's writing, including fiction, non-fiction, novels and screen work.

BEST AMERICAN MYSTERY STORIES OF THE YEAR. (Vol. 1) Edited by Carolyn Wells. The John Day Company: 1931
Contains: "The Farewell Murder"

BEST AMERICAN MYSTERY STORIES OF THE YEAR. (Vol. 2) Edited by Carolyn Wells. The John Day Company: 1932
Contains: "Death and Company"

SHORT STORIES OF TODAY. Edited by Raymond W. Pence. The Macmillan Co.: 1934
Contains: "The Farewell Murder"

THE SMART SET ANTHOLOGY. Edited by Burton Rascoe and Groff Conklin. Reynal and Hitchcock: 1934
Contains: "The Green Elephant" and "From the Memoirs of a Private Detective"

CHALLENGE TO THE READER. Edited by Ellery Queen. Frederick A. Stokes: 1938
Contains: "A Man Called Knott" ("A Man Called Spade")

STORIES FOR MEN. Edited by Charles Grayson. Garden City Publishing Company: 1938
Contains: "Two Sharp Knives"

101 YEARS' ENTERTAINMENT. Edited by Ellery Queen. Little, Brown and Company: 1942
Contains: "A Man Called Spade"

INTRODUCTION TO MODERN ENGLISH AND AMERICAN LITERATURE. Edited by W. Somerset Maugham. New Home Library: 1943
Contains: "A Man Called Spade"

WORLD'S GREAT DETECTIVE STORIES. Edited by Will Cuppy. World Publishing Company: 1943
Contains: "A Man Called Spade"

BACHELOR'S COMPANION. Edited by Burton Rascoe and Groff Conklin. Grayson: 1944
Contains: "The Green Elephant"

BEST STORIES FROM ELLERY QUEEN'S MYSTERY MAGAZINE. Edited by Ellery Queen. Detective Book Club: 1944
Contains: "Fly Paper"

SPORTING BLOOD. Edited by Ellery Queen. Little, Brown and Company: 1944
Contains: "His Brother's Keeper"

AVON ANNUAL: 18 GREAT MODERN STORIES. No editor listed. Avon Books: 1945
Contains: "To a Sharp Knife" ("Two Sharp Knives")

THE BEDSIDE TALES. Edited by Peter Arno. William Penn: 1945
Contains: "Two Sharp Knives"

BEST FILM PLAYS OF 1943–44. Edited by John Gassner and Dudley Nichols. Crown: 1945
Contains: screenplay of "Watch on the Rhine"

GREAT AMERICAN DETECTIVE STORIES. Edited by Anthony Boucher. World Publishing Company: 1945
Contains: "Too Many Have Lived"

ROGUES' GALLERY: Edited by Ellery Queen. Little, Brown and Company: 1945
Contains: "Ruffian's Wife"

THE ART OF THE MYSTERY STORY. Edited by Howard Haycraft. Simon and Schuster, Inc.: 1946
Contains: "From the Memoirs of a Private Detective" and a book review of "The Benson Murder Case"

FOURTH MYSTERY COMPANION. Edited by A.L. Furman. Lantern Press: 1946
Contains: "The Tenth Clue"

HALF-A-HUNDRED STORIES FOR MEN. Edited by Charles Grayson. Garden City Publishing Company: 1946
Contains: "Nightshade"

THE HARD-BOILED OMNIBUS. Edited by Joseph T. Shaw. Simon and Schuster, Inc.: 1946
Contains: "Fly Paper"

MURDER FOR THE MILLIONS. Edited by Frank Owen. Frederick Fell: 1946
Contains: "Two Sharp Knives"

MURDER WITHOUT TEARS. Edited by Will Cuppy. Sheridan: 1946
Contains: "They Can Only Hang You Once"

TO THE QUEEN'S TASTE. Edited by Ellery Queen. Little, Brown and Company: 1946
Contains: "The Gutting of Couffignal"

TWENTIETH CENTURY DETECTIVE STORIES. Edited by Ellery Queen. World Publishing Company: 1948
Contains: "Tom, Dick or Harry"

AS TOUGH AS THEY COME. Edited by Will Oursler. Permabooks: 1951
Contains: "Corkscrew"

THE WORLD'S GREATEST BOXING STORIES. Edited by Harold U. Ribalow. Twayne: 1952
Contains: "His Brother's Keeper"

TEN GREAT MYSTERIES. Edited by Howard Haycraft and John Beecroft. Doubleday and Company, Inc.: 1959
Contains: *The Maltese Falcon*

ELLERY QUEEN'S 16TH MYSTERY ANNUAL. Edited by Ellery Queen. Random House, Inc.: 1961
Contains: "A Man Named Thin"

BIBLIOGRAPHY

MAGAZINE AND NEWSPAPER ITEMS RELATING TO HAMMETT

THIS LISTING DOES NOT COVER all published book reviews on Hammett's work from newspapers and magazines. Only those of major importance have been listed. In order to avoid duplication, certain magazine material by Hellman, Gide, Bazelon, Maugham, Chandler, et al., which was later collected into book format, is listed only in the book section relating to Hammett. Anonymous items are listed chronologically.

Anon. "They Stand Out from the Crowd," *Literary Digest,* December 9, 1933
Hammett as one of a brief series of biographical sketches.

Anon. "Dashiell Hammett Has Hard Words for Tough Stuff He Used to Write," Los Angeles *Times,* June 7, 1950
Syndicated newspaper bit on Hammett. With photo.

Anon. "Obit," New York *Times,* January 11, 1961
A profile of Hammett, which includes quote on the Op.

Anon. "Continental Op," *Newsweek,* July 25, 1966
A review of *The Big Knockover* in which Hammett's detective is discussed. With photo.

Archer, Eugene. "Detective Story," *Films and Filming* (London), September, 1959
Examines "The Maltese Falcon" as part of a monograph on John Huston. Illustrated with stills.

Asbury, Herbert. "Red Harvest," *Bookman,* March, 1929
An in-depth review of Hammett's first book.

Balmer, Edwin. "Our Literary Nudism," *Esquire,* September, 1934
A *Redbook* editor traces the purchase history of *The Thin Man.*

Borneman, Ernest. "Black Mask," *Go* (London), February-March, 1952

A history of the American pulp magazine, with emphasis on Hammett.

Boucher, Anthony. "Woman in the Dark," New York *Times,* August 10, 1952

A review of the Hammett paperback collection.

Caen, Herb. "Nights of Old," San Francisco *Chronicle,* November 26, 1967

Memories of old San Francisco.

Durham, Philip. "Hammett: Profiler of Hard-Boiled Yeggs," Los Angeles *Times,* November 21, 1965

A review-essay, inspired by *The Novels of Dashiell Hammett.* With photo.

Eyles, Allen. "Great Films of the Century: The Maltese Falcon," *Films and Filming* (London), November, 1964

In-depth examination of the Huston/Hammett film. Illustrated with stills.

Fleming, Ian. "Raymond Chandler," *London Magazine,* December, 1959

Reference is made to Hammett in relation to Chandler.

Gardner, Erle Stanley. "Getting Away With Murder," *The Atlantic,* January, 1965

Memories of Hammett and Carroll John Daly.

Gardner, Frederick H. "Return of the Continental Op," *Nation,* October 31, 1966

A review-essay inspired by *The Big Knockover.*

Godfry, Lionel. "Martinis Without Olives," *Films and Filming,* April, 1968

An article on the private-eye image in films.

Goulart, Ron. "The Private Eye," *P.S.*, August, 1966

An essay on the private detective genre, including Hammett.

Haas, Joseph. "The Big Knockover," Chicago *Daily News,* June 18, 1966

A review which links Hammett and Hemingway.

Handlin, Oscar. "Reader's Choice: Dashiell Hammett," *Atlantic Monthly,* July, 1966

A review of *The Big Knockover.*

Harriman, Margaret Case. "Miss Lily of New Orleans," *New Yorker,* November 8, 1941

A profile on Lillian Hellman, mentioning Hammett.

Haycraft, Howard. "From Poe to Hammett," *Wilson Library Bulletin*, February, 1938

A "foundation listing" of detective fiction, in which Hammett is listed as "founder of the modern, hard-boiled, high-speed school of detective writing."

Hellman, Lillian. "Dashiell Hammett: A Memoir," *New York Review of Books*, November 25, 1965

The first printing of what later became the introduction to *The Big Knockover*. With a caricature drawing of Hammett.

——. "The Time of the Foxes," New York *Times*, October 22, 1967

Memories of the opening of her play, "The Little Foxes."

Lyons, Leonard. "Tales About Hammett Told," Hollywood *Citizen-News*, January 19, 1961

A syndicated newspaper memoir by Lyons.

Macdonald, Ross (Kenneth Millar). "Homage to Dashiell Hammett," *Mystery Writers' Annual*, 1964

An article on Hammett's work.

——. "The Writer as Detective Hero," *Show*, January, 1965

An article, with references to Hammett.

Madden, David. "James M. Cain and the Movies of the Thirties and Forties," *Film Heritage*, Summer, 1967

Article on the classic tough-guy films, with stills.

Martin, John Bartlow. "Peekaboo Pennington, Private Eye," *Harper's*, May, 1946

A profile of Pennington, in which a Hammett plot is discussed.

McInnes, Graham. "Elementary, My Dear Watson," *University of Toronto Quarterly*, July, 1947

An essay on the detective genre.

Moss, Leonard. "Hammett's Heroic Operative," *New Republic*, January 8, 1966

A review-essay inspired by *The Novels of Dashiell Hammett.*

Paterson, John. "A Cosmic View of the Private Eye," *Saturday Review*, August 22, 1953

An in-depth essay-history of the genre.

Phelps, Donald. "Dashiell Hammett's Microcosmos," *National Review*, September 20, 1966

A review-essay inspired by *The Big Knockover.*

Queen, Ellery (Frederic Dannay and Manfred B. Lee). "The

Green Elephant," *Ellery Queen's Mystery Magazine*, November, 1945

A preface to Hammett's story, discussing its history. (Contains data not included in any of the Queen-edited Hammett collections.)

Quennell, Peter. "The Thin Man," *New Statesman and Nation* (London), May 26, 1934

A review which favorably compares Hammett to Hemingway.

Redman, Ben Ray. "Decline and Fall of the Whodunit," *Saturday Review*, May 31, 1952

An article on the mystery field, with special attention to Hammett. With photo.

Ruhm, Herbert. "In Rats' Alley," *Carleton Miscellany*, Winter, 1967

A review-essay inspired by *The Big Knockover*.

Sanderson, Elizabeth. "Ex-Detective Hammett," *Bookman*, January-February, 1932

The first in-depth profile of Hammett, with photos.

Schickel, Richard. "Dirty Work," *Book Week*, August 28, 1966

A review-essay inspired by *The Big Knockover*.

——. "Raymond Chandler, Private Eye," *Commentary*, February, 1963

A review-essay inspired by *Raymond Chandler Speaking*, with reference to Hammett.

Shaw, Joseph T. *Black Mask*, February and November, 1927 December, 1929—February and June, 1930

Editorial commentary on Hammett and his work.

Stoddard, Roger E. "Some Uncollected Authors XXXI: Dashiell Hammett, 1894–1961," *Book Collector* (London), Spring, 1962

A biographical-critical profile, with check-list of Hammett's books.

Weisman, Al. "Hammett of Alaska," *Yank*, December 20, 1945

A profile of Hammett in the service during World War II.

BOOK ITEMS RELATING TO HAMMETT

THIS LISTING DOES NOT COVER all volumes which mention Hammett. Excluded are titles carrying only a one-line reference or a simple group-inclusion of his name, and which add nothing of importance to data available elsewhere. Anonymous items are arranged chronologically.

Anon. *Who's Who in America,* Volume 16:1930–1931. A.N. Marquis: 1930

Hammett is included in the entries. (An updated sketch appeared in Volume 25 of this series, published in 1948.)

Anon. *The Smiling Corpse.* Farrar and Rinehart: 1935

In this novel Hammett is included as one of several real people used as fictional characters.

Anon. *Twentieth Century Authors,* edited by Stanley J. Kunitz and Howard Haycraft. H.W. Wilson: 1942

Contains biography of Hammett, with photograph and book-list.

Anon. *Masterpieces of World Literature in Digest Form,* First Series, edited by Frank N. Magill. Harper & Row: 1949

Contains critiques and story plots on three Hammett novels: *The Maltese Falcon, The Glass Key, The Thin Man.*

Anon. *Twentieth Century Authors,* First Supplement, edited by Stanley J. Kunitz. H. W. Wilson: 1955

Updates Hammett biography to 1953, with listings.

Anon. *Cyclopedia of World Authors,* edited by Frank N. Magill. Harper & Row: 1958

Hammett is included among author entries.

Anon. *100 Great American Novels,* edited by Albert H. Morehead and Harold J. Blum. Signet/New American Library: 1966

Contains biographical page on Hammett, and plot of *The Thin Man.*

Angoff, Allan (editor). "The World of the Detective Story," from *American Writing Today.* New York University Press: 1957

Hammett and the hard-boiled school discussed.

B. Ay. *Encyclopaedia Britannica,* Volume 11. William Benton: 1966

Hammett is included among the entries.

Bazelon, David T. "Dashiell Hammett's Private Eye" from *Scene Before You,* edited by C. Brossard. Rinehart: 1955

Bazelon's critical-biographical essay reprinted from May, 1949 issue of *Commentary.*

Becker, Stephen. *Comic Art in America.* Simon and Schuster, Inc.: 1959

Contains reproduction of one of the daily 1934 Hammett/Raymond strips on "Secret Agent X-9," with a history.

Blair, Walter. "Dashiell Hammett: Themes and Techniques," from *Essays on American Literature in Honor of Jay B. Hubbell,* edited by Clarence Gohdes. Duke University Press: 1967

Discusses Hammett's life and work.

Cain, James M. *The Butterfly.* Alfred A. Knopf, Inc.: 1947

In a preface, Cain denies the Hammett/Hemingway influence in his work.

Chandler, Raymond. *Raymond Chandler Speaking,* edited by Dorothy Gardiner and Katherine Sorley Walker. Houghton Mifflin Company: 1962

Chandler makes several references to Hammett in this collection of letters and essays.

——. *The Simple Art of Murder.* Houghton Mifflin Company: 1950

In his title essay (revised from its first printing in *Atlantic Monthly,* December, 1944) Chandler discusses the Hammett influence on crime fiction.

Couperie, Pierre and Maurice C. Horn. *A History of the Comic Strip.* Crown: 1968

Commentary on and illustrations from "Secret Agent X-9."

Crowther, Bosley. "The Maltese Falcon," from *The Great Films.* G. P. Putnam's Sons: 1967

Contains a section devoted to the Huston/Hammett production as "one of the 50 greatest all-time films." With history and plot, including stills.

——. *The Lion's Share.* E. P. Dutton and Co., Inc.: 1957

Contains a film history of "The Thin Man."

Downer, Alan S. "The Monitor Image," from *Man and the Movies,* edited by W.R. Robinson. Lousiana State University Press: 1967

Discusses the Huston/Hammett "Maltese Falcon."

Durham, Philip. *The Boys in the Black Mask.* Privately-printed pamphlet issued by U.C.L.A.: 1961

Discusses Hammett and lists several Hammett items in the U.C.L.A. pulps collection.

——. *Down These Mean Streets a Man Must Go.* University of North Carolina Press: 1963

In this, the only book-length study of Raymond Chandler and his work, Durham makes several references to Hammett.

——. "The Black Mask School," from *Tough Guy Writers of the Thirties,* edited by David Madden. Southern Illinois University Press: 1968

A history of the magazine's chief contributors, with a long section on Hammett.

Edenbaum, Robert I. "The Poetics of the Private Eye: The Novels of Dashiell Hammett," from *Tough Guy Writers of the Thirties,* edited by David Madden. Southern Illinois University Press: 1968

In-depth discussion of Hammett's major novels.

Fadiman, Clifton (editor). *Fifty Years.* Alfred A. Knopf, Inc.: 1965

References to Hammett in Fadiman's introduction and in his preface to Chandler's *Farewell, My Lovely.*

Fiedler, Leslie A. *Love and Death in the American Novel.* Stein and Day: 1960 (Revised Delta paperback edition with new data, 1966)

Hammett and the hard-boiled school are discussed.

Fitzgerald, F. Scott. *The Letters of F. Scott Fitzgerald,* edited by Andrew Turnbull. Charles Scribners Sons: 1963

In a letter written shortly before his death (dated September 14, 1940) Fitzgerald refers to Hammett.

Gardner, Erle Stanley. "The Case of the Early Beginning," from *The Art of the Mystery Story*, edited by Howard Haycraft. Simon and Schuster, Inc.: 1946

Gardner discusses Hammett and the early *Black Mask* days.

Gide, André. *Imaginary Interviews.* Alfred A. Knopf, Inc.: 1944

Discusses Hammett in a section reprinted from the February 7, 1944 issue of *New Republic.*

Goulart, Ron (editor). *The Hardboiled Dicks.* Sherbourne Press: 1965

Goulart's introduction discusses Hammett as part of the history of the pulp-based private eye.

Graves, Robert and Alan Hodge. *The Long Week End: A Social History of Great Britain, 1918–1939.* The Macmillan Co.: 1941 (in U.S.)

Selects Hammett as the most important crime novelist of this period in America.

Grebstein, Sheldon N. "The Tough Hemingway and His Hard-Boiled Children," from *Tough Guy Writers of the Thirties,* edited by David Madden. Southern Illinois University Press: 1968

Links Hemingway with Hammett and Chandler.

Gruber, Frank. *The Pulp Jungle.* Sherbourne Press: 1967

This autobiographical account of the period includes a discussion of Hammett.

Hackett, Alice P. *70 Years of Best Sellers: 1895–1965.* R.R. Bowker Co.: 1967

Contains statistical data on Hammett's two major best-selling novels, *The Thin Man* and *The Maltese Falcon.*

Hagen, Ordean. *Who Done It?* R. R. Bowker Co.: 1969

A comprehensive listing of crime novels.

Harmon, Jim. *The Great Radio Heroes.* Doubleday and Company, Inc.: 1967

Discusses the Hammett radio shows, with dialogue excerpts.

Haycraft, Howard. "America: 1918–1930," from *Murder for Pleasure.* D. Appleton-Century: 1941

Contains a section on Hammett and his part in the development of the detective story.

Hecht, Ben. "Drinking Bout," from *Charlie.* Harper & Brothers: 1957

In this chapter Hecht describes a Hollywood party of 1932, Hammett attending.

Hellman, Lillian. *Six Plays by Lillian Hellman.* Modern Library: 1942

In her introduction to this edition, the playwright discusses her friendship with Hammett. ("The Children's Hour," included in this volume, is dedicated: "For D. Hammett, with thanks.")

——. "Lillian Hellman," from *Writers at Work: Third Series.* Viking Press: 1967

The Hellman interview conducted by John Phillips and Anne Hollander, reprinted from *Paris Review,* Winter-Spring, 1965, in which Hammett is discussed.

Hemingway, Ernest. *Death in the Afternoon.* Charles Scribners Sons: 1932

Hemingway comments on Hammett's *The Dain Curse.*

Herzberg, Max J. *The Readers Encyclopedia of American Literature.* Thomas Y. Crowell: 1962

Hammett is included among the entries.

Hyams, Joe. *Bogie.* New American Library: 1966

Hyams quotes from Richard Schickel on Sam Spade in a section on "The Maltese Falcon."

Legman, Gershon. *Love and Death.* Breaking Point: 1949

Discusses the hard-boiled writers, including Hammett.

Levant, Oscar. *The Unimportance of Being Oscar.* G.P. Putnam's Sons: 1968

Discusses Hammett and Lillian Hellman.

Malin, Irving. "Focus on The Maltese Falcon: The Metaphysical Falcon," from *Tough Guy Writers of the Thirties,* edited by David Madden. Southern Illinois University Press: 1968

Deals with the Hammett novel in metaphysical terms.

Maloney, Martin. "A Grammar of Assassination," from *The Use and Misuse of Language,* edited by S. I. Hayakawa. Harper & Row: 1962

This essay on the mystery discusses Hammett and Chandler.

Maugham, W. Somerset. "The Decline and Fall of the Detective Story," from *The Vagrant Mood.* Doubleday and Company, Inc.: 1953

Discusses Hammett and Chandler.

Noble, Peter. *The Fabulous Orson Welles.* Hutchinson (London): 1956

Relates show-business anecdote involving Hammett.

Nolan, William F. "Bogie and the Black Bird," from *John Huston: King Rebel.* Sherbourne Press: 1965
Contains the history of the Huston/Hammett filming of "The Maltese Falcon."

Queen, Ellery (Frederic Dannay and Manfred B. Lee). *In the Queens' Parlor.* Simon and Schuster, Inc.: 1957
Hammett discussed in several sections.

——. *Queen's Quorum.* Little, Brown and Company: 1951
Lists *The Adventures of Sam Spade* as one of the most important books published in the field since 1845.
Dannay and Lee also contributed introductions and story prefaces to several of their Queen-edited collections. (See BOOKS.)

Rosenberg, Bernard and David Manning White (editors). *Mass Culture.* Free Press/Macmillan, Inc.: 1957
Contains a section, "Detective Fiction," in which Hammett is discussed.

Sandoe, James. *The Hard-Boiled Dick.* Privately-printed pamphlet issued by A. Lovell: 1952
In a "personal check-list" of detective works Sandoe lists Hammett's novels, with comment. (This listing reprinted in *The Armchair Detective,* January, 1968.)

Shaw, Joseph T. (editor). *The Hard-Boiled Omnibus.* Simon and Schuster, Inc.: 1946
Discusses Hammett in his introduction to this collection of *Black Mask* fiction. (Contains a Hammett story from the Shaw period.)

Sinclair, Upton. *100%—The Story of a Patriot.* Sinclair: 1920
This novel contains, as a minor character, a detective named Hammett, and Sinclair notes: "Practically all the characters . . . are real persons."

Thompson, H. Douglas. *Masters of Mystery.* William Collins & Sons (London): 1931
Mention is made of Hammett.

Thurber, James. "The Wings of Henry James," from *Lanterns and Lances.* Harper & Brothers: 1961
Discusses Hammett and James in this essay.

Waugh, Coulton. *The Comics.* The Macmillan Co.: 1947
Includes a history of the Hammett/Raymond strip, "Secret Agent X-9."

BOOKS RELATING TO THE HARD-BOILED SCHOOL OF LITERATURE

For the reader who wishes to trace the roots of this school of writing I would strongly recommend the collection of essays superbly edited by David Madden, *Tough Guy Writers of the Thirties*. And no student of the genre can afford to overlook Howard Haycraft's two major pioneering volumes, *Murder for Pleasure* and *The Art of the Mystery Story*. The collected letters and essays in *Raymond Chandler Speaking* are as valuable and fascinating as Chandler's fiction—and Philip Durham's full-length study of this writer, *Down These Mean Streets a Man Must Go*, is also vital to the history of the tough school. (Full data on these titles may be found in the Hammett check-list.)

In fiction within the field, Ross Macdonald's Lew Archer novels, beginning in the Forties with *The Moving Target*, are all in the Hammett tradition. Paul Cain's ultra-tough *Fast One* (1933) is a prime example of diamond-hard writing, and there are a number of other crime novelists whose best work is worth serious attention: John D. MacDonald, William Campbell Gault, Fredric Brown, Cornell Woolrich, Roy Huggins, Bob Wade and Bill Miller (as Wade Miller), Howard Browne (writing the Paul Pine novels as John Evans), and Donald E. Westlake (writing the Parker novels as Richard Stark). Ian Fleming's James Bond series would qualify as hard-boiled, particularly his very tough *Live and Let Die*.

Raymond Chandler's early novels, featuring Philip Marlowe (*The Big Sleep, Farewell, My Lovely, The High Window*, and *The Lady in the Lake*), were collected by Knopf in 1964, in *The Raymond Chandler Omnibus*. His other three Marlowe novels, *The Little Sister, The Long Goodbye* and *Playback*, in

separate editions, are also essential reading, as are his two main collections, *The Simple Art of Murder* and *Killer in the Rain.* A valuable Chandler collection was published in England (in 1965) as *The Smell of Fear,* by Hamish Hamilton. In it are all the stories from *The Simple Art of Murder,* but this volume also contains Chandler's first and last stories *not* included in the U.S. edition, "Blackmailers Don't Shoot" and "The Pencil."

At least three anthologies are also worth seeking out: Joseph T. Shaw's *The Hard-Boiled Omnibus,* Will Oursler's *As Tough As They Come,* and Ron Goulart's *The Hardboiled Dicks.*

Many of the mainstream novels of the Thirties tied directly into the tough school, beginning with William Faulkner's *Sanctuary* in 1930. Other influential key works of the period: *The Postman Always Rings Twice* by James M. Cain (1934), *They Shoot Horses, Don't They?* by Horace McCoy (1935), *To Have and Have Not* by Ernest Hemingway (1937), *Hope of Heaven* by John O'Hara (1938), *The Grapes of Wrath* by John Steinbeck (1939), and *The Day of the Locust* by Nathanael West (1939).

Other writers who greatly influenced the genre are Nelson Algren, James T. Farrell, Ring Lardner, John Dos Passos, Graham Greene, W. R. Burnett. There are many more. The joy and excitement of rooting them out shall be left to the individual reader. The titles mentioned here (and others within the main text and Hammett check-list) form a necessary foundation, and may be found in most libraries.

INDEX

Index

NOTE: This index covers only the main text (pages 1 through 127). Fictional characters and works (novels, stories, etc.) are listed under the author's name in each case.